STARTING
AND RUNNING
A SMALL BUSINESS

The Bare Facts

REVISED EDITION

ELIJAH M. JAMES, PH. D.

Canadian Cataloguing in Publication Data

James, Elijah M.

Starting and Running a Small Business, Revised

ISBN 978-1-998692-06-4

EJ Publishing

663 White Hills Run

Hammonds Plains

Nova Scotia, Canada. B4B 1W7

This book is dedicated to Koren A. Norton. As a small business owner and manager, you embody resilience, creativity, and the courage to navigate the challenges of building something meaningful from the ground up. Your entrepreneurial spirit and unwavering dedication are an inspiration to all who aspire to follow their dreams. May your journey continue to inspire others to pursue their passions with determination and grace.

TABLE OF CONTENTS

PREFACE

Many decades ago, with some degree of justification, it used to be said that not much written material was available to small and prospective business owners. What was available was largely inaccessible to many small business owners. That state of affairs was unfortunate because the need for helpful information about starting and running a small business has long been acknowledged. Thousands of small businesses fail frequently because of inadequate preparation for becoming small business owners and/or insufficient management skills.

Over the past few years, the situation has changed. Now, there is a sea of information and advice about starting and running a small business enterprise. The problem now is that small business owners and prospective small business owners can be easily drowned in this bewildering sea of information. There are detailed textbooks designed for use in college and university courses dealing with entrepreneurship and small business management, and these serve their purposes. But many small business owners will probably never set foot in one of those classes, and do not have the time to contend with four or five hundred pages of rather technical material.

What is required is a book that presents the *required* material in a non-technical, non-threatening manner. The question is, What is the required material? In my capacity as an economic, business, and management consultant, and as a small business owner, I have been made aware of the basic needs of small business owners. They need information that is necessary to help them succeed in business. They need to know both the personal and business prerequisites for becoming a successful small business owner, and they need to know the basics of small business management. They need this information in a small handy book that is easy to read and goes straight to the bare facts. *Starting and Running a Small Business: The Bare Facts* fills this need.

The book is written specifically for anyone who is involved or plans to be involved with small business ownership or management. Every effort has been made to make this book readable and understandable. The selection of materials to be included was based on the expressed needs of numerous small business owners, coupled with the author's own experience.

Starting and Running a Small Business: The Bare Facts is divided into 16 chapters. The first seven chapters deal with starting a small business, while the remaining chapters deal with running a small business. Chapter 1 outlines the small business environment, while Chapter 2 helps individuals determine whether or not they have what it takes to be small business owners. At a very early stage, the prospective small business owner must decide on the legal form of the business and its location. These topics are dealt with in Chapters 3 and 4. Business success requires planning, so Chapter 5 is devoted to this very important, but often neglected, topic. The best ideas and plans will fail to materialize unless the necessary capital can be acquired. Small business financing is the subject of Chapter 6. The question of staffing the enterprise with competent workers is addressed in Chapter 7.

A business can never succeed unless it can market its product/service, and inappropriate pricing decisions can be fatal for a small business. Chapters 8 and 9 address the issues of successful marketing and pricing. The small business owner needs records and financial statements, without which, he/she will be floundering in the dark. Chapter 10 turns the light on important records for the small business. Chapter 11 shows how to plan for profit, while Chapter 12 deals with budgeting and control. Small businesses face a variety of risks. Chapter 13 shows how to protect against these risks. Chapter 14 deals with credit selling, while Chapter 15 discusses Artificial Intelligence and Small Business. Chapter 16 contains an annotated list of Internet resources for small businesses. A glossary of common business terms is included as a convenient reference.

In the course of writing a book, the author almost invariably amasses huge debts. This particular case is no exception. My Children, Ted and Andrea, have provided a great deal of encouragement during the writing of this book. Without their moral support, the task would have been much more difficult. Thanks guys.

I also express my gratitude to my sister Vera James (Sister V) who painstakingly performed the arduous task of proofreading the entire original manuscript. I thank Constance Simon (Connie) for preparing the original document for publication. I am thankful to Koren Norton and her team for converting the manuscript into a veritable work of art.

Finally, I am greatly indebted to the many scores of small business owners who took the time and interest in this project to verbalize their needs, and whose candid expressions largely dictated the selection of materials to be included in this book. I thank you all.

Elijah M. James

CHAPTER 1

THE SMALL BUSINESS ENVIRONMENT

◈

Introduction

With the unprecedented pace of technological development, more and more small businesses are being established. Witness the proliferation of small home businesses that have sprung up just within the past five years. There is no doubt that small businesses occupy an important place in the economic landscape. On a daily basis, most of us carry on transactions with small businesses — the dry cleaner, the corner grocery store, the photographer, the auto body repair shop, the barber shop, the law firm, the boutique at the corner of Main and Fourth, your friendly neighbourhood florist— just to name a few.

The above are all examples of small businesses. The examples given are small businesses that provide a variety of services to customers, but it should not be inferred that small businesses operate only in the service sector. In fact, many small businesses are in the manufacturing sector with small factories producing windows, doors, cabinets, picture frames, electronic components, jams, souvenirs, and a large variety of other products on a small scale.

Definition of Small Business

The concept of a small business is not easy to define. What may be considered small in one field may be quite large in another, and what may be considered large in one country or region may be quite small in another. The problem is compounded by the fact that some businesses with only a few employees may have very large sales volume, while some businesses with many employees may have relatively low sales volume. It is hardly surprising then, to find that different writers define *small business* differently.

More than 60 years ago, the Committee for Economic Development (CED) defined a small business as one that has at least two of the following characteristics:

- ◆ Management of the business is independent. Usually, the managers are also the owners.

- ◆ Capital is provided by an individual or by a small group of individuals who own the business.

- ◆ The area of operations is mainly local, and the workers and owners live in the same home community. The markets however, need not be local.

- ◆ The business is small relative to the biggest units in the industry. There is great variation in the size of the top bracket, so that what might seem large in one industry would be definitely small in another.

Clearly, the CED's definition allows for a wide variety of businesses of varied characteristics to be classified as small. One problem with this definition, as with any qualitative definition, is that it does not lend itself to sufficient specificity.

To resolve the issue of vagueness, other writers have defined small business in quantitative terms. For example, the Office of Advocacy of the Small Business Administration in the United States seems to define a small business as one that has fewer than 500 employees. Statistics Canada, on the other hand, emphasizes businesses with fewer than 50 employees when discussing small business.

The Australian Bureau of Statistics defines a small business as:

- *Manufacturing businesses employing less than 100 persons; or*

- *Construction & service sector organizations employing less than 20 persons; or*

- *Agricultural firms where the value of agricultural operations is between $20,000 and $4,000,000 per annum.*

The Department of Trade and Industry in the United Kingdom makes a distinction between micro firms and small firms. It adopts the following definition:

Definition	Number of employees
Micro firm	0-9
Small firm	10-49
Medium firm	50-249
Large firm	250 +

Note that a firm with 300 employees in the UK would be considered large, while the same firm in the United States would be classified as small.

It is also possible to define small businesses in terms of sales volume. For example, one could establish an arbitrary upper limit of $2 million in annual sales as the criterion for describing a small business. For our purpose, we define a small business as follows:

A small business is one that has 20 or fewer employees, and annual sales of $2 million or less.

According to this definition, it would probably be more appropriate to employ the concept of a "mini" business or "micro" business. That observation notwithstanding, we have decided to use the more popular concept of small business.

The Small Business Scene

Number of Small Business Enterprises

The number of small businesses in the United States and Canada, using our definition, is not known exactly, but reliable statistics from the U.S. Census Bureau place the number of small firms at about 5.3 million for the United States. The number for Canada is 1.05 million. Many of these firms are operated by single owners with no employees, or with fewer than five employees.

Ownership

In the past, business ownership resided predominantly with men. In recent years, however, that situation has been changing. Whereas in 1979, less than 25 percent of businesses had women owners, by 1996, the figure had risen to more than 33 percent. Interestingly enough, the number of women owners is growing three times as fast as the number of male owners.

As of recent data, the percentage of small businesses owned by women in the U.S., Canada, and the U.K. is as follows:

♦ **United States**: Women own approximately 42% of all U.S. businesses, equating to over 13 million enterprises.

◆ **Canada**: Women majority own about 18% of businesses, including small, medium, and large enterprises.

◆ **United Kingdom**: Women-owned and women-led businesses account for approximately 23.85% of private-sector employment.

These figures highlight the significant contributions of women entrepreneurs to the economies of these countries. Evidently, increasing numbers of women are assuming the entrepreneurial role.

Form of Business

The main forms of business organization under which a firm may be established are a corporation, a partnership, or a sole proprietorship (single entrepreneur). By far, the most popular form of business organization for small firms is the sole proprietorship with over 70 percent of them choosing this form. Only about 22 percent are corporations, and still fewer (7%) partnerships.

Financing

Small businesses are financed mainly by traditional loans at commercial banks. Other important financing sources include personal and business credit cards and finance company credit.

Business Failure

Business failure occurs when a business is unable to sustain its operations because of financial, operational, or market challenges, ultimately leading to its closure or bankruptcy. It typically means the company is no longer able to generate sufficient revenue to cover its expenses, meet debt obligations, or maintain profitability.

Business failure can result from various factors, including poor management decisions, lack of market demand, insufficient capital, intense competition, economic downturns, or external disruptions. It is often measured by the cessation of business activities, legal insolvency, or the inability to satisfy stakeholder expectations.

Business failure seems to be one of the trademarks of small businesses. Data from the United States and Canada suggest that the failure rate among small businesses is quite high, especially within the first five years of operation. Determining business failure rate is a difficult task largely because of the definition of failure. For example, one can obtain statistics on business closures, but these statistics may not apply to business failure. A firm may close for many reasons not related to business failure.

Wage Profile

If you intend to keep wage costs down by hiring mainly minimum wage earners, then you'll be going against the norm. Small firms have a lower tendency to hire minimum wage earners than do large firms. Statistics indicate that only 17 percent of micro-businesses employ workers at minimum wage, compared to 23 percent for large firms.

Job Satisfaction

Job satisfaction seems to be higher among employees of small firms than among employees of larger firms. The small business scene seems to offer more flexibility and higher employee morale than larger businesses.

More Hours but Less Money

Small business owners tend to work longer hours but typically earn less money than paid employees. A work week of more than 50 hours is not unusual among small business owners. More than 25 percent of business owners generally work more than 55 hours per week, compared with only three percent of paid workers. Although business owners usually work more hours than paid employees, they typically earn only slightly more than 75 percent of the income earned by paid employees.

Profitability

Profit is a strong incentive for owning a small business. However, small businesses seem to earn less profit than larger businesses. On an annual basis, large businesses show a return of about 6 percent on their assets. The comparable figure for small businesses is 4 percent.

The Tax Scene

Taxes seem to impose a tremendous burden on small businesses. In Canada, the most harmful taxes to small businesses seem to be local property and business taxes, workers' compensation premiums, personal income taxes, and employer health taxes.

Reasons for Starting a Small Business

As we have hinted earlier, the number of people who have ventured into the small business ownership field is significant. In Canada, the United States, and the United Kingdom, many new business owners are new immigrants, following their displacement from their home country. Another explanatory factor is the tremendous support that is now provided to small businesses by governments. Yet another reason for starting small businesses is the vast amount of information, guidance, and other resources now so easily and readily available to would-be entrepreneurs.

Many people enter the small business world because they were terminated from their employment, possibly with sufficient funds to enable them to become self-employed. There are many other reasons for starting a business, and you probably have your own to add to the list. According to the Small Business Administration (SBA) in the United States, some of the most common reasons for starting a business are the following:

- ♦ You want to be your own boss.

- You want financial independence.
- You want creative freedom.
- You want to fully use your skills and knowledge.

In a study of women business owners in Atlantic Canada by Jody Manly and Joanne Gallivan, the authors noted that women tend to start businesses for personal reasons such as the challenge offered or the opportunity for self-fulfilment, rather than for financial reasons. According to the said study, factors that have considerable influence on women's decision to start a business include:

- an opportunity to be one's own boss
- personal accomplishment
- perceived opportunity in the marketplace
- balancing work and family
- flexibility regarding work conditions
- lack of employment options.

Advantages of Owning a Small Business

Small business ownership has several important advantages for the owners. Among them are the following:

Sense of Accomplishment

Small business ownership gives the owners a sense of accomplishment. They tend to feel that they have achieved something worthwhile, and that gives them a feeling of self-fulfilment.

Independence

Small business ownership confers a certain degree of independence. You are your own boss and your employment and progress at work are not dictated by the whim or fancy of an employer. You have an opportunity to make independent decisions from which you derive some measure of satisfaction.

Possibility of Future Wealth

As a small business owner, you have the prospect of future wealth. Many small business owners have reaped substantial financial rewards for their efforts and are able to enjoy considerable wealth and financial security as a result. Wouldn't it be nice to be numbered among them?

Personal Exposure

Small business ownership affords you the chance of personal contact with customers, workers, and other business owners. It gives you a high profile in the community and much greater visibility than might otherwise be possible.

Personal Development

Being the owner of a small business helps you develop a variety of business and social skills. You learn bookkeeping, marketing, public relations, purchasing, and a wide variety of other skills. You learn how to conduct yourself at certain functions, and you acquire the social graces that are becoming a small business owner.

Challenge

If you relish a challenge, you will find it as a small business owner. Just making a go of it is a challenge in its own right. As a small business owner, you can count on facing at least one new challenge each day.

Entrepreneurial Prestige and Pride

A certain amount of prestige is associated with small business ownership. You would be hard-pressed to find a small business owner who does not exhibit pride in being able to say. "I am my own boss." Often, when someone enters a small business establishment and asks, "Who is the owner?" The reply: "I am the owner" is often uttered with transparent dignity and unbridled pride.

Psychic Income

The term "psychic income" refers to the non-financial benefits derived from engaging in certain activities. They can be considered as intrinsic rewards. Many small business owners could probably earn more income as employees, but they prefer to remain small business owners because of the enjoyment they experience. Small business ownership confers psychic income.

Disadvantages of Owning a Small Business

Small business ownership does not come without its disadvantages and limitations. It exacts a price. Below we highlight the downside to owning a small business.

Risk of Failure

Small business ownership carries a high risk of failure with its concomitant loss of funds. Some observers and students of small business problems claim that the small business failure rate may be as high as 4 out of 5 in some industries. Irrespective of the definition or measure of business failure that is used, the failure rate for small businesses seems relatively high. Entrepreneurship can be a risky business.

Demanding

We indicated earlier in this chapter that small business owners tend to work long hours. Entrepreneurship demands a commitment of time. This factor has consistently ranked high as a disadvantage of small business ownership. It seems that owning and running a small business leaves little time to pursue other activities and interests. You must be willing to make the sacrifice.

Skill Requirement

Owning a small business often requires a wide variety of skills — a variety that is unlikely to reside in any single person. The small business owner will often be required to possess record-keeping skills, recruiting and selection skills, human and public relations skills, bill collection skills, inventory management skills, and the list goes on.

Family Problems and Stress

Because of the great demand that small business ownership places on the entrepreneur's time, less time is available to spend with the family. Family problems such as separation and divorce are not unusual among small business owners. Owning your own business is stressful and can therefore be a cause of health-related problems.

Economic Significance of Small Business

If you are already a small business owner, or if you decide to become one, you should be aware of the economic contribution that you are (or will be) making as a small business owner. Let us briefly discuss the economic significance of small business by examining the following six key areas.

- ◆ Employment and job creation
- ◆ Output
- ◆ Wages and salaries
- ◆ Profits
- ◆ Exports
- ◆ Training and Research and Development

Employment and Job Creation

The evidence is conclusive that small firms collectively employ huge amounts of people. Small businesses are vital contributors to employment across the United States, Canada, the United Kingdom, and Australia. Here's an overview of their impact:

United States: Small businesses employed an estimated 56.4 million workers in 2021.

Canada: Small businesses (1–99 employees) accounted for 97.8% of all employer businesses as of December 2022.

United Kingdom: Small businesses provide nearly 44% of all jobs in the UK.

Australia: Small businesses employ over 5.1 million people, underscoring their role as the backbone of the Australian economy.

These figures highlight the significant role small businesses play in providing employment and driving economic growth in these countries.

Output/Sales or Receipts

In the Australian economy, small businesses employing fewer than 20 employees account for almost 30 percent of total output. The comparable figure for firms with more than 500 employees is about 29 percent. In the United States, employer firms with fewer than 20 employees have annual receipts of over $2,805 billion. This is a significant contribution to the economy.

Wages and Salaries

In addition to hiring employees and selling goods and services, small businesses contribute to the economy by paying wages and salaries and making other payments on behalf of their employees. The annual payroll of firms with fewer than 20 employees in the United States is estimated at just over $1 trillion.

Profits

Clearly, not all small businesses are profitable; otherwise, the failure rate among small firms would be lower than it actually is. Had it not been for the prospect of profits, many small business owners would not have exposed their resources to risk, and economic activity would be at a lower level.

Profit margins for small businesses vary significantly across industries and countries. Here's an overview of average profit margins in the United States, Canada, the United Kingdom, and Australia:

United States: The average profit margin for small businesses is approximately 7%.

Canada: Profit margins vary by industry. For example:

- *Primary Care Doctors: 42.1%*
- *Agriculture and Forestry: 8.4%*
- *Construction: 4.6%*
- *Manufacturing: 2%*
- *Wholesale and Retail Trade: 2%*
- *Professional and Technical Services: 6.3%*

United Kingdom: Profit margins for small businesses vary widely depending on the industry. For instance, service-based industries such as consulting or legal services can have up to 70% gross profit margins.

Australia: A good profit margin for small businesses typically falls between 10% to 20%, though this can vary by industry.

It's important to note that these figures are averages and can vary widely depending on the specific industry, business model, and economic conditions. Service-based industries often have higher profit margins compared to manufacturing or retail sectors because of lower overhead costs.

Exports

Although small businesses do not contribute as much to exports as do large firms, they still play an important role. Small businesses with fewer than 20 employees account for about 15 percent of total exports. As increasing numbers of small businesses turn their attention to e-commerce, the share of small businesses in the export trade will likely increase.

Training and Research and Development

The role of training and research and development (R& D) in the economy should not be underestimated. Training increases the efficiency of workers, and R&D leads to innovation, product development, and improvement. Small firms that are growing seem to spend more on training than their medium-sized counterparts. In addition, small firms seem to spend as much as three times more on R&D than large firms.

Conclusion

You should now have a clear picture of the small business environment and of some of the conditions under which you will have to operate your small business. As an entrepreneur, you can make a significant contribution to the economy in terms of providing employment opportunities and creating new jobs, creating new products and services, and encouraging greater efficiency and productivity. Other people will play a role in determining whether or not you will succeed, but it is you who will play the major role in determining your success or failure. Small business ownership can be exciting and always challenging. The next chapter will discuss the personal and other requirements for success as a small business owner.

CHAPTER 2

BEFORE YOU BEGIN

Introduction

You have what you consider to be a terrific business idea. It's a "fresh" concept, and no one else you know of has thought of it. What do you do? Do you just "run with it?" Or, you have acquired a good amount of money and it has always been your dream to own your own business, to be your own boss. Now you can afford it. Where do you go from here? This chapter explains the steps you should take before you actually become a small business owner — one who is successful, anyway.

Even if you are already a small business owner, you can still benefit from the contents of this chapter. For example, we discuss several requirements for success as a small business owner. If you already own your own business and do not possess the requirements for success, then you may be able to take the necessary steps towards acquiring what it takes.

Do You Have What It Takes?

Many business failures can be avoided if those who are contemplating small business ownership take the time to determine whether or not they have what it takes to succeed as a small business owner. Well, you are bent on being a successful small business owner. That's why you bought this book, and that's why you will pay careful attention to the advice and instructions given in this chapter. Right? Let's look at some of the most important requirements for small business success. First, we will look at some of the personal attributes that are required for success, and then we will consider other key requirements.

Personal Attributes for Success

Dedication

Success as a small business owner requires patience, stamina, and dedication. Small business ownership is not a "get rich quick" scheme. It requires *sticktoitability* (stick-to-it-ability) — the ability to stay with it. If you are willing to give up at the first sign of difficulty, then perhaps you don't have what it takes to be a successful business owner. Dedication does not suggest foolhardiness. You must have the good sense to know when to give it up when it's just not working out.

Ability to Work Long Hours

In the previous chapter, we indicated that small business owners work long hours. Are you prepared to spend the time that is necessary to get the desired results? If a 9 to 5 job is more to your liking and you just can't afford to spend long hours building your business, then perhaps you should get a 9 to 5 job as an employee and give up the idea of small business ownership.

Willingness to Take Risk

Entrepreneurs are risk-takers. If you are entirely averse to risk-taking, then the entrepreneurial world is not for you. Small business ownership is a risky business. If you have some financial resources that you are not prepared to expose to risk, then you should place them in some very safe assets such as savings accounts at commercial banks, most probably at relatively low returns. You must be reminded that in general, the higher the risk, the higher the returns. Does this mean that you have to be a big-time gambler? Not really. The risk that we are talking about is calculated risk.

Leader or Follower

Some people are leaders, while others are followers. Some people enjoy making independent decisions, while others would rather not make one but sit on the proverbial fence. If you want to become a successful small business owner, you have to be capable of making decisions. You may, of course, obtain information and guidance, but you have to be able to make independent decisions. You must be able to accept the leadership role.

Ability to Plan Ahead

There is not a great deal of room for mistakes in small businesses. No one is perfect, so you will make mistakes. However, you can minimize the occurrence of these mistakes by planning. If you know what is likely to emerge in the future, you can prepare yourself to deal with it. If you are a person who has difficulty planning, you are not likely to succeed as a small business owner.

Flexibility

If you are a rigid and unchangeable individual, you are not suited for an entrepreneurial role. Small businesses must be able to adjust to the changing needs of their customers and to changing market conditions.

As a small business owner, you must be able to adapt to changing conditions if you are to be successful.

Ability to Face Challenges

Small business ownership presents constant challenges to the entrepreneur. The ability to face these challenges is a major requirement for success as a small business owner. Careful planning will help to alleviate some of these challenges but it will not eliminate them entirely. Many of these challenges will be of crisis proportions, so be prepared.

Emotional Fortitude

Running a small business can be emotionally draining. Many small business owners have succumbed to the emotional strain and have had to bow out. Do you have the emotional strength to be a small business owner? If you crack easily under pressure, it may be a signal that you lack the emotional fortitude that is necessary for success in the small business arena.

Other Important Requirements

Pertinent Skills

Contrary to popular opinion, many small business owners have college training and university degrees. However, the higher education that they possess may not be directly related to small business ownership. Take a moment to reflect on the skills that you will need to run a small business, and then ask yourself, "Do I have the pertinent skills?" It is unlikely that you will possess all the pertinent skills, but you must be able to find personnel with the required skills.

Capital

It requires capital to start a business. It's good that you have a superb business idea, but unless funds are available to make that idea a reality, it will remain just that – a superb idea. Determine as precisely as possible how much money you will need to start the business, and then establish whether or not such funds are available or can be acquired.

The Business

In my capacity as a consultant, I have met many people who want to enter the field of small business ownership. You might be surprised to know that many of them don't know what kind of business they want to get into. It's important to spend enough time determining what kind of business is right for you. If you don't like to meet and interact with people, then perhaps a travel agency may not be the right kind of business for you.

What is your product or service? Are you going to be a manufacturer or retailer? Where will you get your supplies? Where will be a suitable location for your business? These are all important questions that you need to answer *before* you actually start the business.

Feasibility Study

Conducting a feasibility study is a rather technical undertaking, but it's an exercise you need to do before you launch out into small business ownership. A feasibility study will help you to answer the following question: Does this business idea or proposal have a good chance of success?

The following are among the questions that will be raised and answered by a feasibility study.

- ◆ Do I know exactly what business I want to enter? What product do I want to sell or what service do I want to provide?

- ◆ Who will be my customers?

- ◆ Why would people buy my product or service?

- Do I have a suitable location for my business in terms of accessibility, traffic, public utility services, etc.?

- Who will be my suppliers? Are they reliable?

- How stiff a competition will I have to face? Are any competitors serving the market well? What advantages do I have over them? (Superior location, lower price, better service, etc.)

- What personnel will I need to produce the product or to offer the service? Will adequate staff be available?

- Will my product/service satisfy a need that is not presently being served?

- Is my target market being served adequately?

- Is the start-up capital requirement reasonable or highly excessive?

- Will adequate financing be available?

- Will I be able to market my product/service effectively?

- What is the least amount of money I must make from this business venture to make it worth my while?

- How much money will I need to invest in the business?

- How much could I earn by investing this money elsewhere?

- What is the typical return on investment (ROI) in the type of business that I am contemplating?

- Does my pro forma (projected) income statement indicate that my business will be profitable? What profit margin can I expect?

- How large is the market that I will serve?

- What share of this market can I realistically expect to capture?

- Is this market growing or shrinking?

- Are my prospective clients particularly price-conscious? Why would they be willing to pay my price?

- Has any new business entered the market recently? Has any left recently?

- Who has the largest share of the market?

- What advertising and promotional media will be most effective for my business?

- Will I be able to obtain credit from my suppliers? What are their terms?

- Am I aware of the major risks that I will face? Can I protect myself against these risks?

If you cannot conduct a feasibility study for yourself, find someone competent who can. It is better to bear the cost of a good feasibility study than the pain of thousands of dollars going down the drain on a business that had no chance of success in the first place. A good feasibility study can save you a bundle.

Business Plan

Whereas a feasibility study will tell you if your business has a good chance of succeeding, a business plan is like a road map telling you how to get from where you are to your desired destination. The feasibility study tells you whether or not the business *can* be successful. The business plan tells you what you must do to make the business successful. The business plan provides some assurance of success.

Why You Need a Business Plan

Many people believe that you need a business plan only to raise money. That is a misconception. Although a business plan is an important instrument in raising capital, it performs a variety of other important functions.

Giving Direction You wouldn't think of embarking on a long journey in an automobile to some unfamiliar destination without a current road map or a global positioning system (GPS) to guide you. The same should apply to your business. You need a plan to guide you.

Acquiring Capital Although some individuals can start a business without borrowing, many people will need to borrow. Today, lenders such as banks and other financial institutions are requiring you to have a business plan before they even consider an application for a loan. Lenders want to be certain that you know where you are, where you want to go, and how you plan to get there.

Keeping You Focused The business plan helps you to focus on every aspect of your business – financing, advertising and promotion, your competitors, your market, staffing, customer relations, etc. It also forces you to get the necessary information on which important business decisions will be based.

Exercising Control You will need to control your business operations – costs, inventory, purchasing, etc. The business plan will help you establish the necessary mechanisms for effective control.

Arranging Financing Your business plan will force you to carry out the exercise of determining your capital requirement, where the money will come from, exactly what it will be used for, and how you plan to repay any loans.

Self-Assessment Worksheet

There are several self-evaluation tests designed to help you decide whether or not you have attributes commonly found in successful entrepreneurs. Bear in mind that some people have done extremely well on these tests, yet they fail as small business owners. Others perform poorly on the tests, yet go on to become rather successful small business owners. Does this mean that these self-evaluations are useless? Certainly not. One big advantage of such tests is that they help you focus on some of the characteristics of successful small business owners.

Assessment Questionnaire

Evaluate yourself by placing an X in the appropriate box on the right.

[Yes] [No]

1. Are you a tenacious person by nature, holding fast to your ideas and convictions?

[Yes] [No]

2. Do you have the patience to see something through to the end once started?

[Yes] [No]

3. Do you like to take things as they come, and just adjust?

[Yes] [No]

4. Do you enjoy taking charge of situations?

[Yes] [No]

5. Do you prefer to allow someone else to take charge and then join in with your support?

[Yes] [No]

6. Do you enjoy relying on the know-ledge and experience of others?

[Yes] [No]

7. Do you have a tendency to accept situations as they are?

[Yes] [No]

8. Do you like high risk situations just for the thrill?

[Yes] [No]

9. Do you try to avoid interacting with unfamiliar people?

[Yes] [No]

10. Do you accept defeat graciously?

[Yes] [No]

11. If you fail at something, is it easy for you to try it again?

[Yes] [No]

12. Is it important for you to be your own boss?

[Yes] [No]

13. Do you try to avoid challenging situations?

[Yes] [No]

14. Do you try to succeed by any means necessary?

[Yes] [No]

15. Have you ever been involved in any community project?

[Yes] [No]

16. Do you have a small business ownership background?

[Yes] [No]

17. Do you often offer suggestions about how things can be improved?

[Yes] [No]

18. Are you usually perceptive about solutions to problems?

[Yes] [No]

19. Are you prepared to sacrifice time with family to be successful in your business?

[Yes] [No]

20. Have you had a history of poor health?

[Yes] [No]

21. Did you take an active part in extra curricular activities at school?

[Yes] [No]

22. Did you do odd jobs when you were in your early teens (lawn mowing, for example)?

[Yes] [No]

23. Would the lack of a college or university degree deter you from owning your own business?

[Yes] [No]

24. Do you enjoy job situations where you have considerable latitude to make your own decisions?

[Yes] [No]

25. Do you think you can fail without being defeated?

[Yes] [No]

26. Are you willing to spend a great deal of time to accomplish a goal?

[Yes] [No]

27. Do you feel it's a waste of time to try something at which many have failed?

[Yes] [No]

28. Do you require a good amount of sleep (more than 9 hours) each night to be able to function properly?

[Yes] [No]

29. Are you generally self-reliant?

[Yes] [No]

30. Do you want to own your own business because of the status and power it confers?

[Yes] [No]

Answers to Assessment

Correct responses to the following questions should be **Yes**.

1,2,4,6,11,12,15,16,17,18,19,21,22,24,25,26,29.

Correct responses to the following questions should be **No.**

3,5,7,8,9,10,13,14,20,23,27,28,30.

Determining Your Score

In order to determine your score, assign one point for each correct answer. If your score is between 20 and 30, you have most of the characteristics and attributes common among successful entrepreneurs. A lower score does not mean that you won't succeed as a small business owner, but it means that your attributes, outlook, and views differ from most of those found among successful entrepreneurs. Similarly, a high score is not a guarantee of success as an entrepreneur.

CHAPTER 3

CHOOSING
THE LEGAL STRUCTURE

Introduction

You are now familiar with the small business environment; you have satisfied the preconditions for entering the world of small business ownership — checking personal attributes, feasibility study, business plan, etc. — and you are now ready to take the plunge, so to speak. If you have not already done so, you will have to choose a legal form of organization for your business.

This chapter discusses the various legal forms from which you may choose, along with the advantages and disadvantages of each. It also provides some hints as to when incorporation may be a good option. An outline of a Partnership Agreement is included.

The Variety of Legal Structures

Most small businesses are sole proprietorships. The reasons for the prevalence of the sole proprietorship form of business organization should become obvious as we examine each of the legal structures. Deciding on the appropriate legal structure for your business is an important matter and should not be taken lightly. It might be a good idea to consult a professional such as an accountant, a consultant, or a lawyer who has expertise in this field.

The most common legal structures for small businesses are: single or sole proprietorships, partnerships, and corporations. Let us examine each in turn.

Sole Proprietorship

Of the three types of legal structures mentioned, the sole proprietorship is the simplest and easiest to establish. It is inexpensive and can be set up rather quickly. In this legal form of business, you are the sole owner, and you are entirely responsible for the financing of the business as well as for all its debts. On the upside, you enjoy all the profits.

Advantages of the Sole Proprietorship

This legal form of business organization has several advantages, among which are the following:

Fast and Relatively Easy to Set Up In general, sole proprietorships are faster and easier to set up than corporations. Consequently, it is generally less expensive to set up a sole proprietorship than a corporation or even a partnership.

Significant Freedom from Regulations The sole proprietorship has minimum legal regulations. Although you still have to file certain reports with the government, these are a great deal fewer than in the case of a corporation. Thus, the time and expenses involved are less.

Tax Benefit The sole proprietorship form of business organization *may* enjoy some tax advantages. For one thing, the business itself pays no income tax, but the owner pays tax on the income earned from the business. Also, this form of business organization allows you to write off *reasonable* business losses against your personal income. This facet is an attractive feature, especially since losses are quite common in the infant stages of many small businesses.

Being Your Own Boss Those who derive a certain amount of pride from being their own boss will find that the sole proprietorship form of business provides it. You can spend as little or as much time as you please developing and running your business, but you must remember that the decisions you make have consequences. For example, spending too little time attending to your business might spell business failure. Moreover, being your own boss does not rid you of your responsibilities to your customers, and you must still comply with government regulations.

Ownership of All Profits Any profits that a sole proprietorship may earn accrue exclusively to the owner. The single proprietor does not have to share the profits of the business with partners as is the case of a partnership, or with other shareholders as is the case of a corporation. You, and you alone, reap the benefit of your hard labour.

Disadvantages of the Sole Proprietorship

Despite its many advantages, the sole proprietorship form of business organization suffers some disadvantages.

Unlimited Liability First and foremost is the fact that this structure operates under *unlimited liability*. This simply means that the sole proprietor is fully liable personally for all the debts of the business. In this regard, he/she can lose his/her personal assets, including savings and real estate. In other words, there is no legal distinction between your business assets and your personal belongings in this form of business organization.

Difficulty in Raising Capital Another problem that sole proprietors face is difficulty in raising capital for their businesses. Single entrepreneurs have to rely on their own resources, whether owned or borrowed. If huge sums of money are required, the single owner may not be in a position to raise the necessary amount. This partly explains why single proprietorships tend to remain small; and as a small operator, you may not be able to take advantage of benefits such as quantity discounts.

Limited Ability Quite often, the sole proprietorship will suffer from a lack of certain abilities and skills. The single owner is responsible for all aspects of the operation of the business — inventory purchase, selling, accounting, manufacturing, marketing, human resource management, insurance, etc. It is unusual to find one individual who is endowed will all these skills. It's not easy being Jack or Jill of all trades.

Lack of Continuity The single entrepreneur suffers from a lack of continuity. Uncertainty about the continuation of the business following the untimely or unexpected removal of the single owner by death or otherwise may create problems for the firm. For example, creditors may be reluctant to extend credit under such conditions of uncertainty.

Partnership

A partnership is a form of business organization in which two or more people (the partners) agree to unite for the purpose of conducting business. The agreement may be oral, written, or merely a matter of understanding between the partners.

Partnership Agreement

It should be pointed out that a written partnership agreement is not a legal requirement for the formation of a partnership. However, one of the best pieces of advice that can be given about a partnership is that the agreement should be in writing. Even with relatives and good friends, experience has taught that it is advisable to draw up a partnership agreement.

A partnership agreement should contain the following:

(a) the names of the partners

(b) the capital to be contributed by each partner

(c) the manner in which profits are to be distributed among the partners

(d) the duration of the agreement

(e) management duties

(f) provision for dissolution.

The following is an outline of a typical partnership agreement.

Outline of a Partnership Agreement

PARTNERSHIP AGREEMENT

This Partnership Agreement is made in three (3) original copies on the _____ day of _____, 20____ between:

John Peters of Mississauga, Ontario; Norma Williams of Brampton, Ontario; and Alan Henry of Toronto, Ontario. *(Names are fictitious)*

1. PARTNERSHIP NAME AND BUSINESS

The partners agree to form a Partnership under the name of _____ to carry on a business of _____.
The principal place of business of the Partnership shall be _____.

2. TERM

The Partnership shall begin on _____day of _____, 20____ , and shall continue until terminated as provided in this agreement.

3. CAPITAL

Each partner shall contribute $_____ in cash to the Partnership no later than the _____ day of _____,20____, and no partner shall withdraw any part of his/her contribution. If further capital is required, the partners agree to make additional contributions in equal amounts as required.

4. PROFITS AND LOSSES

The net profits of the Partnership shall be divided equally among the partners, and the net losses shall be sustained equally by the partners. An income account shall be maintained for each partner, and profits and losses shall be credited or charged to each partner's income account. If a partner has no credit balance in his/her income account, losses shall be charged to his/her capital account.

5. SALARIES AND DRAWINGS

No partner may receive a salary for services rendered to the Partnership, but each partner may, from time to time, withdraw the credit balance in his/her income account.

6. INTEREST

Partners are not paid any interest on their initial contributions to the capital of the Partnership or on any subsequent contributions of capital. However, if a partner makes a *loan* to the Partnership, he/she is entitled to interest at the going market rate.

7. MANAGEMENT DUTIES AND RESTRICTIONS

All partners shall have equal responsibility for the management of the Partnership business, and shall devote their entire ordinary working time to the running of the business. No partner shall borrow or lend money, or make, deliver, or accept any commercial paper, or execute any mortgage, security agreement, bond, or lease, or purchase or contract to purchase, or sell or contract to sell any property for or of the Partnership other than the type of property bought and sold in the regular course of its business, without the prior consent of the other partners.

8. BANKING

The partners shall maintain a bank account in the name of the Partnership business at a convenient branch of the _____ Bank on which cheques may be drawn on the signature of any two of the partners.

9. BOOKS

The Partnership books shall be maintained at the office of the Partnership, and the partners shall at all times maintain full and proper accounts of the business. All partners shall, at all times, have access to the books.

10. FISCAL YEAR END

The fiscal year end of the business shall be December 31 each year.

11. VOLUNTARY TERMINATION

The Partnership may be dissolved at any time by agreement of the partners, or by any partner giving written notice to the other partners of his/her intention to dissolve the Partnership. Upon dissolution of the Partnership, the assets of the Partnership shall be liquidated and applied in the following order:

(a) to pay the liabilities of the Partnership;

(b) to refund any outstanding additional advances;

(c) to the credit balances of the partners' income accounts;

(d) to the credit balances of the partners' capital accounts.

12. DEATH

Upon the death of any partner, the surviving partners shall have the right to purchase the interest of the decedent in the Partnership, or to terminate and liquidate the Partnership business.

13. ARBITRATION

Any controversy between the partners arising out of or related to this Agreement shall be referred to and settled by a single arbitrator agreed upon by all the partners. The decision of the arbitrator shall be final and binding on the partners.

14. JURISDICTION

This Agreement is governed by the laws of the Province of _____.

Executed on the ___ day of _____, 20___ in_____.

_____   _____

Partner   Signature

_____   _____

Partner   Signature

_____   _____

Partner   Signature

There are two types of partnerships — the general partnership and the limited partnership. In a *general partnership*, all partners are jointly and severally liable for the debts of the partnership, meaning that each partner is responsible not only for his/her own debts but also for the debts of the entire business. In a *limited partnership*, some partners are liable only for the level of their investment in the business. Such partners are called *limited partners*. Limited partners are not supposed to be involved in the management of the business. There must be at least one general partner. The following discussion refers to the general partnership.

Advantages of the Partnership

The following are among the advantages of the partnership.

Greater Availability of Capital Two or more people are likely to be able to raise more capital than a single owner can. By pooling their financial resources, the partners may be able to raise more funds for expansion, for example, than may be the case with a single owner.

Tax Advantage Like the single proprietorship, the partnership is not subject to income tax. Individual partners, of course, must pay taxes on their incomes, but the partnership itself pays no tax on its earnings.

Possibility of Better Business Decisions Knowing that each partner is jointly and severally liable, they are likely to engage in discussion before any important business decision is made. Such discussions are likely to lead to more sober decisions than those reached by single proprietors who do not need to engage in such discussions. There is an old saying that two heads are better than one, even when the subject is lettuce.

Broader Talent Base The partnership may benefit from the variety of special abilities and skills possessed by the partners. One may have expertise in accounting, another in customer relations, another in marketing, another in management, etc., all contributing to the successful operation of the business.

Disadvantages of the Partnership

The partnership form of business organization overcomes some of the problems of the single proprietorship, but it has certain serious disadvantages. The following are a few of them.

Lack of Continuity Lack of continuity, cited as a disadvantage of the single proprietorship, applies also to the partnership. If one partner dies or if agreement cannot be reached among the partners, the partnership may have to be dissolved. Thus, the partnership has a limited life.

Difficulty in Raising Additional Capital The partnership is likely to be able to raise more capital than can the single proprietorship. However, there is still a serious limitation to the amount of capital the typical partnership can raise.

Unlimited Liability The partnership is not a legal entity distinct from the partners. Each partner is individually liable for the debts of the partnership because the partnership does not have limited liability. A bad business decision by one partner may put the personal assets of the other partners in jeopardy.

Corporation

A corporation is a form of business organization in which the owners have limited liability. Limited liability means that the owners are liable for the debts of the corporation only to the extent of their investment in it. Thus, the personal assets of the owners are protected.

The corporation is a legal entity, distinct from its owners. The owners of the corporation are called shareholders or stockholders. The corporation, as a legal entity, may buy, sell, and own property in its own name. It may enter into contracts, sue, or be sued. The corporation may be viewed then as a legal person with its own rights, duties, and responsibilities.

Advantages of the Corporation

There can be little doubt or debate that the corporation has several important advantages. The following are some of these advantages.

Ability to Raise Money The corporation has a tremendous ability to raise large sums of money. You will recall that difficulty in raising funds was one of the problems faced by single proprietors and partnerships. By selling shares, the corporation can raise funds, and the shareholders are assured that in the worst-case scenario, they can lose only the money invested.

Potential for Perpetual Life The lack of continuity that was cited as a problem with single proprietorships and partnerships does not apply to the corporation. If the owners (shareholders) die, the corporation continues as a legal entity.

Specialized Management The corporation can usually afford to hire the services of competent managers. It can hire a staff of researchers, accountants, lawyers, economists, and other business professionals.

Easy Transfer of Ownership The shares of the corporation can easily be transferred from one owner to another. If shareholders want to relinquish their ownership, they can do so simply by finding a buyer.

Limited Liability This aspect of the corporation is one of its most attractive features. Shareholders are liable only to the extent of their investment in the business. They are said to have limited liability. If the business fails, the shareholders' liability is limited to the amount of money they spent in buying shares in the business.

Disadvantages of the Corporation

The disadvantages of the corporation include the following.

Double Taxation Unlike the single proprietorship and the partnership, the income of the corporation is taxed twice. The corporation pays a tax before its profits are distributed to its shareholders, and the amounts distributed to shareholders, that is, their dividends, are subject to taxation.

Close Regulation Of all the forms of business organization, the corporation is the most tightly regulated. There are numerous government regulations, including the necessity of obtaining a government charter, governing the operation of corporations. Complying with these regulations can be both time-consuming and costly.

Loss of Control The shareholders may have little or no control over the operation of the corporation, and its managers may have objectives that are different from those of the owners.

Wedge Between Labour and Management The size of the corporation often forces a wedge between labour and management, and may also destroy the close personal relationship between owner and customer that is typical of the single proprietorship. It must be pointed out, in all fairness, that this is more a problem of size than of the form of business organization.

When to Incorporate

The notion that small businesses are single proprietorships while large firms are corporations seems to be widespread. While it is true that the vast majority of small businesses are single proprietorships, there is no legal reason why small businesses cannot be incorporated. In fact, it is this author's view that not enough small businesses avail themselves of the advantages of incorporation.

Although it is difficult to lay down hard and fast rules as to when a business should incorporate, the following general guidelines should be helpful. It may be advisable to consider incorporation as a suitable option under the following circumstances.

1. *There Is a Need to Raise Large Sums of Money* The Corporation is unparalleled in its ability to raise capital.

2. *Your Business Requires That You Have Many Creditors* If you must have many creditors in the ordinary course of conducting business, it may be advantageous to incorporate.

3. *There Are Tax Advantages* You should carefully consider the tax implications of incorporating your small business. A good tax accountant or a lawyer who is versed in business taxes will be able to help you determine whether there are tax advantages to be realized by incorporating your small business.

4. *You Are Liable to Be Sued* If you are in a business where the probability of being sued is high, you should consider incorporating your business as a form of protecting your personal assets.

CHAPTER 4

BUSINESS LOCATION

Introduction

An important decision that you will have to make is where to locate your business. Many small businesses fail simply because enough attention has not been given to this important facet of setting up a business. A location that is ideal for one type of business may be inappropriate for another type of business. We can think of cases where small businesses have flourished by moving from a poor location to a more favourable location.

In this chapter, we shall discuss some important considerations that you, a small business owner, should bear in mind when selecting a location for your business. We will raise some issues that will help you to determine what constitutes a good as opposed to a poor business location.

Location Versus Site

It is sometimes convenient to distinguish between location and site. *Location* refers to the general area (country, region, province, city) within which your business activity will take place. *Site* refers to the specific address (street and building) where your business will be situated. Both location and site are important factors in the success of the business. For the purpose of this discussion, we shall use the term "location" to include both location and site.

Importance of Location

A small business owner operated a music store successfully for many years in the commercial district of a city. He bought a large house in a residential area and decided to move the store to his home in order to avoid the rent he was paying. It did not take long for him to realize his mistake. Location is important.

Factors such as inexpensive rent, available space, and proximity to one's home, may not be sufficient to constitute a suitable location. A poor location can cause tremendous hardship for a new firm and may even be the main cause of failure. Too many small businesses with great potential for success have bitten the dust because of poor location. Choosing a good location should be an integral part of the planning process before entering into small business ownership.

Location for Service Businesses

Service businesses include TV and radio repair shops, photocopy services, shoe repair shops, appliance repair shops, travel agencies, car rental services, dry cleaners, etc. TV and radio repair shops do not need a location that offers high visibility. The same applies to appliance repair shops. What they require more than high visibility is a convenient place to carry on their repairs. They find their customers by advertising. It is therefore not necessary to rent space in a luxurious building in the middle of town with its concomitant high rent.

Photocopy services will find good locations in shopping malls that are frequented by large numbers of people, and near colleges and universities where there are large numbers of students who use photocopy services. Shoe repair shops may also find good locations in or near shopping malls. They don't usually need luxurious space, but traffic flow is of prime importance.

Travel agencies and other service businesses that rely on drop-in traffic require locations with heavy pedestrian traffic. Locations on busy street corners are ideal for such businesses.

Car rental services will find offices at airports and areas close to hotels to be good locations. A dry-cleaning business requires a location with easy access and heavy traffic. Other considerations in finding a good location for a service business are:

- parking facilities
- access by public transportation
- possibility of erecting a sign
- neighbouring businesses
- proximity to competitors
- lease arrangements

Since lease requirements and signalization are quite often neglected in considerations of locations for small businesses, we shall briefly discuss the importance of these two factors.

The lease arrangements associated with any given site are of particular importance to a new entrepreneur. The new small business has an uncertain future. It is probably unwise for a new small business owner to saddle the new business with a long-term (five years or more) lease.

It is probably a better idea to seek a one or two-year lease with a renewable clause. Although you may enter the business with great optimism, you would not want to be faced with a five-year lease if the business has to be terminated after one or two years.

Signalization is important for new businesses because a visible and conspicuous sign helps to inform the public of your existence. One sign maker cleverly advertises his business this way: "A business without a sign is a sign of no business." The author has advised many small business owners against renting space in places where they were not allowed to put up signs indicating their businesses.

Location for Retail Businesses

The location of a retail business can be the difference between success and failure, therefore it is a matter that should be given due care and attention. The city or town in which you live might be your first choice in which to locate your retail store, and there may be good reasons for this choice. Perhaps you have many friends and relatives there; you may be well-known. But that particular city or town may not be the only one in your district. Before you decide, you need to investigate the following factors.

1. Population

Collect information about the population of the area in which you plan to set up your business. Find out whether the population is growing, stationary, or declining. Find out the size of the population and the average income in the area. This will give you some ideas about possible demand for your goods or services. A small and declining population with a declining average annual income does not seem to be a favourable site for your business. On the other hand, a rapidly growing population with a large base and increasing average income is closer to the ideal situation.

Study the spending habits of the people in the area that you plan to serve. If you are planning to sell gardening equipment and supplies, you need to find out whether the people live in houses with gardens and lawns, or whether they live mainly in apartment buildings. These are important considerations.

2. The Industrial Situation

You will need to know whether industries are moving into the area or moving out of the area and whether existing industries are expanding or contracting. Industries provide employment and hence income for the people in the area. Industrial expansion is a good sign of future economic prosperity and may be an indication of the suitability of the area for your retail business.

3. Related Facilities

You will need to consider what facilities are important to the success of your retail business and whether those facilities are available in the area you are considering. Questions that you will need to answer include the following. Are banking facilities available? Will you be able to find reliable suppliers? Does the municipality have a pro or anti-business stance? Will you be able to find the kinds of workers you need? Is there a good public transportation system? The importance of the answers to these questions depends on how important they are to your particular retail business.

What about parking facilities? Is there easy parking or will your customers consider it a nuisance to find parking space? If the latter is the case, then you must consider the impact that it will have on your retail business.

4. Competition

You will need to study your contemplated area to determine the extent of competition that you will face. If there are competitors and they are inefficient and not serving the market well, then you will have an easier time dealing with them and making inroads into the market. On the other hand, if they are providing a valuable service and doing it well, your task will be much more difficult.

In studying the competition, you should do so in terms of market size also. If there is already a store similar to the one that you plan to establish in the area, is the market large enough to accommodate two such stores? Clearly, the answer to this question is important in determining whether or not you should be located in that area.

5. Pedestrian Traffic

A good location for a retail business is one where pedestrian traffic is heavy. But you must be concerned with more than the heavy pedestrian traffic. You need to know whether or not these people are potential customers. It does you no good if one million vegetarians per day pass by your butcher store.

6. Affinities

In considering the site for a retail store, you should try to find a location that has businesses that are complementary to yours. Some types of businesses will attract customers to your store. You should be aware of such *affinities* as they are called. The following table identifies good neighbouring businesses for certain types of retail businesses.

Retail Business Affinities

Type of Retail Business	Good Neighbouring Stores
Variety store	Women's clothing, shoe, jewelry, department
Department store	Women's clothing, variety, shoe, men's furnishing
Florist	Restaurants, drug, shoe

Type of Retail Business	Good Neighbouring Stores
Furniture	Men's furnishing, women's clothing, shoe
Women's clothing	Department, shoe, variety
Men's furnishing	Theatres, restaurants, shoe
Candy store	Jewelry, florists, variety
Paint store	Furniture
Pharmacy	Anywhere except near furniture stores
Curtain store	Furniture
Men's clothing	Men's furnishing, jewelry
Woman's hats	Variety, women's clothing, shoe, department.

7. Neighbouring Buildings and Surroundings

When considering a site for your small retail business, you must study the neighbouring buildings and surroundings. Depending on the nature of your business and the types of customers you intend to attract, you may want to avoid locations that are near cemeteries, car repair shops, certain types of factories, and slaughterhouses, as such sites may be unattractive to certain types of customers. Neighbouring buildings that have been unoccupied for a considerable length of time may not be particularly good neighbours for your retail business.

Location for Manufacturing Establishments

If your small business enterprise is a manufacturing establishment, and if your objective is to maximize profits, you cannot ignore location factors. In many North American cities, there are zoning laws that restrict manufacturing to certain industrial localities. Usually, however, you will have several industrial zones from which to choose. Once the decision is made, you have to turn your attention to the following factors that may affect your business.

1. Availability of Raw Materials

The availability of the raw materials that will serve as the inputs in producing your product is an important consideration. It is a good idea if you can locate near the source of these materials as this would reduce transportation costs. Additionally, you should consider the availability of semi-finished goods that you will need to manufacture your product. Of course, you will need to consider not only the availability but also the quality and relative costs of these required inputs.

2. Availability of Power and Water

Many manufacturing processes require both electrical power and water. Gas, gasoline, diesel, and coal may also merit consideration. Where several types of power sources are available, cost and reliability might be determining factors.

3. Workers

You will want to locate in an area where the types of skills that you will require are available; otherwise, you may have to bring in workers with the related higher cost. It is clearly an advantage to be able to recruit workers who already live in the area where you plan to locate.

You will also need to get information on the going wages and salaries for the types of workers that you will need since that will help to determine your labour cost.

4. Transportation

An important consideration in selecting a site for your manufacturing establishment is transportation facilities. Will you be transporting your finished product by rail, ship, truck, or air? The answer to this question will determine the ideal site as far as transportation is concerned.

A Final Word

The decision regarding the location of your small business will be guided primarily by cost considerations. In the manufacturing process, three distinct cost elements can be identified: the cost of obtaining raw materials, the cost of manufacturing the product, and the cost of distributing the product to your customers. These cost elements will play an important role in determining the ideal location for your manufacturing establishment.

CHAPTER 5

SMALL BUSINESS PLANNING

Introduction

At some point in your life as a small business owner, you will likely require a business plan. Some small business owners wait until they face a situation in which a business plan is requested before they even think of preparing one. Then they scurry about trying to find someone who can put a plan together at short notice. That is unfortunate.

A business plan should be considered as part and parcel of the requirements for operating a successful small business. You should not confuse a business plan with a feasibility study discussed in Chapter 2. Whereas a feasibility study tells you about the probability of success of your business, a business plan is a guide that should help you to achieve your objectives. The plan tells you what you must do to make the business successful.

In this chapter, we will discuss what a business plan should contain. The preparation of a business plan is a serious undertaking, and much thought should be given to it. For the small business owner, being involved in the process of preparing a plan is even more important than the final resulting document which is called the business plan.

Definition

A business plan is often likened, and with much justification, to a road map. If you are driving to an unfamiliar destination, you will rely on a road map (if one were available) to guide you and to get you there. Well, think of a business plan as your business road map that will lead you through the operation of your business.

We define a business plan as a written document that describes, in significant detail, the various aspects involved in establishing a new business. The plan answers three basic questions: (1) What is my present situation? (2) Where do I want to go? (3) What's the best way of getting there?

Creditors such as bankers, suppliers, and investors will often insist on seeing your business plan. But you must realize that the business plan is not intended only for these groups. It is intended as a guide for you, the business owner.

The business plan can be viewed as one end result of the planning process. Planning is the process by which the new business owner will determine how the business will accomplish its long-term objectives. This type of planning is called strategic planning and it is to this type of planning that we refer in this discussion.

Be Involved in Preparing the Plan

Ideally, the business plan should be prepared by you, the business owner. Unfortunately, the preparation of a good business plan requires certain skills that you may not possess. Therefore, it may be necessary for you to engage the services of a consultant to assist you in preparing the plan. Keep in mind the purpose for which the plan will be used. A plan designed primarily for your own personal use may not require the professionalism required by investors and bankers. In any event, it is of critical importance that you are involved in the preparation of the plan. There are many small business associations and groups that can provide guidelines on the preparation of a business plan.

The Importance of a Business Plan

In Chapter 2, we discussed why you should go through the trouble of preparing a business plan. In this section, we continue that discussion by examining some other aspects of the importance of a business plan.

In this author's opinion, the most important reason for preparing a strategic business plan is to ensure the success of the business. A business plan is important because it helps you to view the whole picture before you make huge commitments of funds. It points out difficulties that you are likely to encounter and how you might deal with them.

A strategic business plan is important because it helps you develop business goals and objectives and forces you to express them in writing. Without clearly defined goals and objectives, the way forward will be hazy and cloudy. A plan clarifies these goals and objectives and helps you to determine exactly what methods will be used in accomplishing these goals and objectives.

Your Mission Statement

Your small business should have a clearly defined mission, otherwise, you will simply be moving about aimlessly. The mission defines your business, so to speak. It tells what business you are in and states the main purpose for which the business exists. A mission statement should be an integral part of any strategic plan.

A retail store that specializes in fashionable clothes for teenage girls states its mission as follows:

Our mission is to provide teenage girls with the most up-to-date fashions in clothes at reasonable prices.

Note that this mission statement identifies the intended customers ("teenage girls"), the firm's product (up-to-date clothes), and a suggestion of a pricing strategy (reasonable prices). This mission statement distinguishes this particular retail store from others of its type.

It is not only profit-oriented organizations that require mission statements. A particular not-for-profit elementary school's mission statement is given below.

The mission of the school is to provide all students with a strong educational program which will facilitate their intellectual, moral, physical, social, and emotional development. We strive to prepare our students to become responsible citizens through the cooperative efforts of the home, school, and community.

Note again that this mission statement defines the fundamental purpose that sets this school apart from others of its type. The school's reason for existence is quite clear.

What Your Plan Should Contain

To a certain extent, the content of your business plan is dependent upon the main purpose it is intended to serve. If you are starting your business with your own money, then your plan need not emphasize how you intend to finance a loan. As a general rule though, the main parts of the business plan can be divided into four distinct sections as follows:

1. Business description
2. Organizational plan
3. Marketing plan
4. Financial plan

Let us examine each of these sections in order.

Business Description

In describing your business, you should be specific about what business you are in. A mission statement (discussed earlier) helps to accomplish this task. As part of the business description, you should state the following:

- Type of business (i.e., whether manufacturing, retailing, service, etc.)

- Form of business organization (i.e., whether single proprietorship, partnership, or corporation), and why you chose that form

- The product or service that you will sell

- The main customers you will serve

- Your business hours

- The goals of your business and why you think you can achieve these goals

- Your business location (Any advantages such as accessibility, traffic flow, security features, etc.)?

Organizational Plan

In this section, you need to show that adequate thought and consideration have been given to the organization and management of the business. The success of your business depends crucially on the type of management it will receive. The organizational plan should indicate:

- ◆ your personal background and experience in this kind of business

- ◆ your personal strengths and weaknesses and steps that you will take to remedy any weaknesses

- ◆ your management team and the backgrounds of its members

- ◆ any gaps in management areas and how they will be remedied

- ◆ management responsibilities (who will be responsible for what)

- ◆ job descriptions

- ◆ board of directors (if a corporation) and the background of each director

- ◆ key employees other than the management team

- ◆ personnel requirements

- ◆ recruiting, hiring, orientation, and training plans

- ◆ wages and salaries, employee benefits, vacation, etc.

- ◆ outside expertise such as consultants, lawyers, accountants, etc.

Investors and creditors will look very closely at the quality of management that you plan to put in place. They know also that your employees play a vital role in the success of the business. The organizational plan is therefore very important.

Note: It's a good idea to include an organization chart.

Marketing Plan

Some small business owners develop a separate marketing plan as a 'stand-alone' document. This allows them to go into significant detail about every aspect of their plans to market their products or services. Whether or not you decide to follow this route, the strategic business plan should still contain a marketing plan.

To be successful as a small business owner, you must market both your business and your product or service. In a later chapter, we will examine methods and techniques for marketing your business. Successful market planning demands that you know your customers' needs and wants, and involves the development of strategies that will allow you to satisfy those needs and wants.

Your marketing plan should include the following:

- ◆ *Industry analysis.* You should present a brief analysis of the industry to which your business belongs. Is the industry expanding or contracting? Can you estimate the future demand for your product/service? These are important issues.

- ◆ *Your customers.* To whom specifically will you sell your product/service? Are they mainly male or female? What is their age range? Where do they live? What is their income? Why will they buy your product/service?

- ◆ *Target market.* Describe the condition of your target market. Is your target market growing rapidly, or slowly or is it holding steady? Is it declining?

- ◆ *Strengths and weaknesses.* What will be your major strengths and weaknesses in this market and how will you compensate for the weaknesses?

- ◆ *Opportunities and threats.* What opportunities will be available to you and how do you plan to capitalize on them?

What are the possible threats that your businesses will face and how do you plan to deal with them? What are the risks and how will you try to minimize them?

- **Market share.** Here you should state your anticipated share of the market on entering the market. You should also indicate how your market share is likely to change over time.

- **Your competition.** The following questions should be answered in this section. What firms compete in this market? Who are your nearest three competitors? Who will be your closest competitor? What advantages do your competitors have over you? What advantages do you have over them? What is the probability of new entrants into the market and how will you deal with this possible threat?

- **Possible technological changes.** We live in a society in which technological changes occur at a rapid pace. Although it is difficult to accurately predict these changes, you should be prepared for them and be able to assess the impact that they will have on your business. The plan should help to protect you from being taken by surprise.

- **Advertising and promotion.** Without customers, you will not be able to sustain your business. Your marketing plan should spell out your plans for advertising and promoting your product/service.

- **Pricing strategy.** You should be familiar with various pricing strategies and decide on one that will help you achieve your firm's objective. New business owners often find it difficult to decide on an appropriate price to charge for their products/services. But this decision is crucial to the success of your business. This section should provide answers to the following questions. What is your pricing strategy and why have you chosen that strategy? Is your price competitive? Is it above or below that of your main competitors?

Note: Your pricing strategy should be consistent with the image that you are trying to maintain. However, remember that a price that is too low may not earn sufficient profits, while you may price yourself out of the market by charging a price that is too high.

Financial Plan

If your objective is to run a profitable business, then solid financial management must be a given. Careful financial planning is necessary if you are to achieve your financial obligations. You will find that most investors and creditors will go straight to the financial section of your financial plan. They are interested in information regarding the financial viability of the business.

Whatever else your financial plan may contain, it must contain the following essential elements.

Start-up budget. You cannot open a business without first incurring some expenses. You should show the amount of money that you will need to open your business, indicating what the money will be used for. Your start-up budget should consist of items such as the following:

- ◆ equipment
- ◆ utilities
- ◆ advertising and promotion
- ◆ organization and administration fees
- ◆ project management fees
- ◆ supplies
- ◆ down-payments
- ◆ licences and permits

- insurance

- legal, accounting, and other professional fees

Operating budget. Unlike the start-up budget which consists generally of once-and-only-once costs, the operating budget consists of expenses that are necessary to keep the business going. Your operating budget should include items such as:

- wages and salaries

- rent

- supplies

- advertising and promotion

- insurance

- loan financing

- accounting and other professional fees

- payroll expenses

- taxes

Projected income statement. A projected income statement for at least three years into the future will reveal how profitable the business is expected to be. The income and expenditure figures contained in the income statement should be realistic.

Projected balance sheet. A balance is a useful financial statement showing the firm's assets (what it owns), liabilities (what it owes), and net worth (the difference between assets and liabilities. The information is helpful in determining the firm's ability to meet its debt obligations. The projected balance sheet should be for a period of at least three years into the future.

Cash flow statement. Like the income statement and the balance sheet, the cash flow statement is an essential feature of the financial plan. The cash flow statement will tell where you plan to get the cash from, and what you plan to do with it.

Note: Unless you have some accounting background or experience, it may be necessary to obtain help in drawing up these financial statements.

Capital requirements. Your financial plan should state the amount of capital required and the time frame within which it is required. For example, out of a total capital requirement of $500,000.00, you may require $150,000 within the next six months.

Use of funds. What will the funds be used for? A look at your start-up and operating budgets will help to answer this question. The information here should be specific rather than general. For example, instead of saying "purchase of furniture and equipment," it is better to say "purchase of a desk, two chairs, and one computer."

Payback strategy. This section, as the name suggests, explains how you plan to pay back any loans you may be seeking, and how dividends will be distributed to shareholders if your business is incorporated.

Presentation of Your Business Plan

Some people believe that the longer the business plan, the better it is. This is an erroneous belief. Your business plan should be sufficiently detailed to provide all the necessary information, but few people will take the time to read a business plan that is 300 pages in length. There is no specific rule that can be given for the length of a strategic business plan for a small business. It depends on the nature of the business and the purpose for which the plan is intended. Generally, a business plan of the type we are discussing here should not run more than 100 pages of normal type on 8.5" by 11" size paper. Business plans with fewer than 50 pages are quite common.

Cover Page

This page contains the name of the business, the title "Business Plan," the period covered by the plan, the name of the person or group to whom it is submitted (if applicable), and the date. An example of a Cover Page is illustrated on the following page.

SMART COPY SERVICE

BUSINESS PLAN

2025-2029

PRESENTED TO:

CSS FINANCIAL GROUP

November 15, 2000

Table of Contents

The Table of Contents follows the Cover Page. It is a convenient device because it allows the reader to find information in the business plan quickly.

Executive Summary

Following the Table of Contents is the Executive Summary.

The Executive Summary highlights the main sections of the business plan. It should provide readers with sufficient information to enable them to decide whether or not they have any interest in the project. Precision should be the hallmark of the Executive Summary. Although it is presented at the front of the business plan document, the Executive Summary should be written after the plan itself has been written.

Body of the Plan

After the Executive Summary, the body of the business plan containing the various sections outlined above is presented.

Appendix

Any information not contained in the body of the plan, but which you think will be of interest to the readers, may be presented in an appendix at the end of the document. Such information may include relevant graphs and charts, brochures, examples of advertising scripts, contracts or agreements, and quotations from contractors or suppliers.

CHAPTER 6

FINANCING
YOUR SMALL BUSINESS

Introduction

You've come up with this great business idea. It's a new concept in service of some sort. You've discussed it with a few trusted friends and they are really excited about it. You've had the feasibility study done, and the business plan is lying on a small table beside your bed. From all appearances, this business idea is a sure winner. There is only one *small* problem. O.K., it's really a **BIG** problem. You don't have the capital to make your 'can't miss' idea a reality.

There is a Biblical reference to the necessity of counting the cost before embarking on a project. A person who starts to build without being able to finish more than the foundation becomes the laughingstock of the community. The same would apply to one who starts a business without making provision for funding.

There are different ways of financing a new business, and the main purpose of this chapter is to acquaint you with some of these sources of funds. Depending on your particular circumstances, some financing sources may be more appropriate than others. All financing sources are not equally desirable. In fact, some of them may be totally unacceptable.

Our focus here is on new business financing, but much of the discussion will apply to existing businesses that may need capital for expansion or other purposes.

The Need for Capital

Clients often approach our consulting firm, requesting assistance in raising capital to get projects off the ground. "If I can just get enough money to start I'll be O.K." is a common refrain. Statements of this nature arise from a misconception of the need for capital. Many new business owners believe that they need capital only to start up the business and that thereafter, the business will generate enough money to eliminate all future capital needs. This view is erroneous.

Another frequent misconception encountered is that only enervated businesses require additional capital after the initial start-up investment. The fact is, that vibrant businesses that are experiencing rapid growth often need additional capital, and it seems that as the business grows, so does the need for capital. Let us briefly examine some of the causes of the need for more capital so that you will not be caught unprepared. The list is by no means exhaustive.

Growth in Sales

As the growth in sales increases, you will require a greater inventory volume to service the greater sales volume. Moreover, as the business grows, you will require more money to pay additional staff, acquire more space, pay for transportation, etc.

Tardy Payments by Customers

If you operate on a credit basis, financial difficulties may cause your customers to delay their financial obligations to you. That means that cash inflow will be slower than anticipated, giving rise to a need for cash.

Financial Mismanagement

This, of course, will not apply to you. Right? But let us mention it anyway, just so that you will be kept on guard. Failure to manage funds efficiently will often lead to the need for additional funds. The simple principle is, if you waste it you'll tend to want it. Careful financial management and control are necessary for successful business management.

Economic Downturns

The economy tends to go through alternating periods of prosperity and depression. During a period of slow or no economic growth, unemployment and falling incomes may reduce your sales and profits. This will give rise to a temporary need for cash.

New Business Opportunities

In the ordinary course of business, new opportunities may present themselves. Such opportunities may require a second store or office in a new location, new equipment, the introduction of a new product or service, etc. It will require capital to take advantage of such opportunities.

Low Level of Retained Earnings

Retained earnings are portions of the profits that are kept back in the business instead of being distributed. Clearly, if the level of retained earnings is too low, it will create a need for additional funds.

Sources of Capital for Small Businesses

It may not be necessary for you to abandon your dream of owning your own successful small business because of a lack of funds. Let us investigate possible sources of capital for your small business. We may group these sources into three broad categories: your own funds, debt capital, and equity capital.

Your Own Money

Perhaps a rich aunt or uncle has left you a bundle in her/his will. Some of this could be used to finance your new business. Or perhaps, a more likely scenario, you were able to put away some funds in a savings account — funds that you can now access to help finance your new business.

Financiers and investors are encouraged when you invest your personal funds in your business. Their reasoning is as follows: If you are convinced that the project is potentially so economically viable, why wouldn't you want to risk some of your own money? A typical question that investors will ask is, "How much money is the owner putting up?" Food for thought, indeed!

Once you have invested your own money, additional capital, for whatever reason, can be obtained either from internal sources or from external sources. As the terms imply, internal sources of capital are sources within the business, while external sources are those outside the business such as lenders and investors.

Internal Sources of Capital

Retained Earnings

This is the main source of internal funds for most businesses. In fact, there are many businesses that use retained earnings to finance all their capital needs. Good financial management dictates that, to the extent possible, sufficient funds be retained from profits to finance the growth of the business.

The great advantage of using retained earnings to finance capital needs is that the funds are there. There is no need to go outside the business to seek funds. A second advantage of this source is that it does not affect the ownership or control position of your business. A third advantage of retained earnings as a source of capital is that there is no loan to be repaid.

Existing Assets

It may be possible to liquidate some assets to satisfy short-term capital needs. An insurance company was able to raise a significant amount of money by mounting an effective campaign to collect outstanding premiums. Other assets that are currently non-productive may be sold to raise short-term capital. For example, one company was able to raise over $12,000 by selling a truck that it had not used for over eight months. Indeed, effective asset management can add significant amounts of cash into the coffers of the business.

External Sources of Capital

Let us now turn our attention to the many sources of capital that are outside the business.

Debt Capital (Loans)

There are many people today who frown on the idea of borrowing money. Some of them may even quote Shakespeare: "Neither a borrower nor a lender be..." or the Bible: "... the borrower is servant to the lender." However, borrowing money is a proven method of financing a business, and it's a source that you may want to consider. In fact, many firms exist for the sole purpose of lending money. The following are some sources from which you may be able to borrow.

Relatives and Friends This may be a good source from which you can obtain the necessary funds to make your business idea become a reality. Friends and relatives may be only too eager to help you realize your dream, especially if they believe in you and think that your idea is worth their financial and moral support.

If the amount of money that you require is not substantial, and if it is difficult to secure funding elsewhere, then this source may be a good alternative. On the downside, borrowing money from relatives and friends to invest in your business could cause a severe strain on the relationship if the business happens not to fail. This is a consideration that you cannot afford to overlook.

Before you borrow money from your relatives and friends, be sure that you provide them with the necessary facts, including, of course, the risks to which their money will be exposed. People who are not familiar with business undertakings often think that once they lend you money, they are automatically part owners and should therefore have a say in how the business is run. These issues should be resolved before you accept their money.

You should make clear that the money is a loan. A good idea is to draw up a loan agreement stating how and when the loan will be repaid. This immediately sets the loan on a business rather than a social setting.

Credit Cards Many small businesses are able to obtain credit cards. This is actually a form of pre-authorized credit. If your business is very new with no track record, it may be difficult to obtain a business credit card. However, you can use your personal credit card.

The usual prudence about credit card use applies here. You can use your credit card to purchase supplies, equipment, etc. But remember that credit cards should be used only for short-term expenses that you'll be able to settle quickly. And don't forget that the interest rates on credit cards are extremely high.

Business Line of Credit (BLC) You'll probably find a business line of credit more palatable than a credit card as far as financing your business is concerned. When you obtain a line of credit, a credit maximum is established. You can draw against this limit as needed. In this sense, a business line of credit resembles a credit card, but the rate of interest associated with a line of credit is much lower than that associated with credit cards.

A business line of credit can be used for purchases that may be too large for a credit card, depending on the maximum amounts of the line of credit and the credit card. When income is not expected to follow expenditure closely, a business line of credit can be used to fill the temporary gap in cash.

The drawback is that a business line of credit is usually available only to well-established businesses with a demonstrated and proven history of profitability. A new business may therefore not qualify.

Commercial Bank Loans Commercial banks are heavily involved in extending loans to businesses. It's a major part of their operation. Many of these banks have special loan programs designed to assist small businesses. If you can convince the banker that you have a sound financial plan, and that the probability of defaulting on a loan is extremely low, and if you can provide adequate collateral, then you may be able to obtain a loan to finance your new business.

There is a popular saying that banks lend money only to people and businesses that don't need it. What is suggested by this saying is that if one could satisfy the prerequisites for the acquisition of a loan, one would not need the loan. The truth of the matter is that banks do not want to expose themselves to undue risk.

If you are relatively new to the bank, or if you have not established a sound credit history, the bank may require a co-signer as a guarantee that the loan will be repaid. The interest rate on commercial bank loans is usually lower than that on a line of credit.

Note: Other financial institutions such as trust companies and credit unions do extend loans to small businesses.

Mortgage Loans Mortgage loan companies and trust companies extend mortgage loans as an integral part of their business. Simply put, a mortgage is a loan secured by property. If the borrower defaults on his/her payments, the creditor may sell the property and apply the proceeds from the sale to the loan.

If you have a mortgage of $100,000 on a property that is valued at $250,000, you may wish to consider an additional mortgage loan of $30,000, say, to finance your business. Such second mortgages as they are called are sometimes used for small business financing. If you opt for a mortgage loan, you must be aware that the mortgaged property is at some risk.

Business Development Bank of Canada Canadian small business owners have access to several small business loan programs through the Business Development Bank of Canada (BDC). Among them are the following:

Young Entrepreneur Financing Program

The objective of this program is to give new small business owners between the ages of 18 and 34 some financial assistance in establishing their businesses.

Term Loans

The money that you can borrow under this scheme can be used for a wide variety of business purposes, including business expansion, acquisition of fixed assets, purchase of existing businesses, and the provision of working capital.

Micro Business Program

Under this program, a new business can borrow up to $25,000 while an existing business can borrow up to $50,000. To minimize failure, the program also offers personalized management support, including two years of follow-up mentoring.

Capital for Aboriginal Entrepreneurs

If you are an Aboriginal entrepreneur, you may want to consider the Growth Capital for Aboriginal Business. This program provides access to capital to start a small business or to expand an existing one, whether on or off a reserve.

The Small Business Loans Act The Small Business Loans Act (SBLA) is a program of the Canadian Federal Government that allows new and existing small businesses to have access to term loans for purchasing and improving fixed assets. The maximum amount that can be borrowed under this Act is $250,000, and in order to qualify, your revenue must be under $5 million.

Small Business Administration Loans American small business owners may obtain loans under guarantees from the Small Business Administration (SBA). The SBA does not itself grant loans but merely guarantees loans made by commercial banks and other lending institutions and agencies, up to certain limits.

If you just fall short of qualifying for a traditional loan, a SBA loan might be just right for you. The Microloan program may be appealing to you, a new small business owner. It's a good way to begin building a good credit track record.

Trade Credit Suppliers of small businesses often extend short-term credit to their customers. For example, when you purchase supplies, you may receive an invoice that must be paid sometime during the next 30 days. Moreover, it is often possible to arrange payment over a longer period such as 60 days. Although this accommodation does not provide cash per se, it does free up cash that can be used for other purposes.

Equity Capital

In debt financing, you retain full and complete ownership of your business. In equity financing, you actually sell a part of your business to investors in exchange for the money you need to start and run the business. There are many types of investors, and their objectives might be different. But none of them will be willing to give you money for nothing. They expect a return on their investment. Let us examine some of the main sources of equity financing.

Angel Investors (Angels) Don't let this name fool you. These are not investors sent from heaven to bail you out financially and then accept a 'thank you' as a reward. Angels invest in businesses, usually at the start-up phase, and may keep a watchful eye over you to ensure that you make wise business decisions. They want to make sure your business succeeds so that they can get their share of the profits.

If your financing requirement is well under $100,000 and you can't raise it from your personal resources, then you might want to consider using this source.

Venture Capitalists Venture capitalists usually have, or have access to, huge sums of money that they are willing to invest in highly profitable, fast-growing business ventures. They are interested in businesses that show great profit and explosive growth potential and offer high and quick returns on investment. Venture capitalists often have a take-over attitude, and before you know it, you may lose control of your business. If control of the business is less important to you than getting the capital, then perhaps this might be worth your consideration.

Private Placements In a private placement situation, you sell shares in your corporation to a select group of individuals. This is not a public sale, so you can decide to whom you will sell shares, and how many investors you want. Also, you decide exactly how much of your company you want to sell and at what price.

It may be possible to get private investors that you know to buy shares in your company even in the beginning stages. It is easier, however, to interest private investors in a venture that has established a track record of profitability and successful operation. A private placement requires good salesmanship if it is to be successful.

CHAPTER 7

YOUR EMPLOYEES

Introduction

Your employees are your most valuable asset. This opening statement has become a cliché, but clichés don't exist without merit. It is unlikely that your small business will be successful unless you have employees who are competent and willing to work for the advancement of the business.

A common cry among small business owners is that they have difficulty finding good workers. This, in itself, may be interpreted as a realization by small business owners that good workers are essential to the success of their business. It is hardly a secret that unreliable, dishonest, lazy, and impolite employees have led to the ruination of many small businesses.

A business needs to be adequately and appropriately staffed. If there are not enough employees, customers may have to wait in long lines before being served, and they will be dissatisfied. If there are too many employees, your wage bill will be bigger than it ought to be, and such unnecessary expenses will have negative effects on your profit margin.

In this chapter, we will discuss a variety of issues that you will find both important and useful in helping you to use your labour resources to achieve your business objectives. You will have to decide exactly what jobs you need workers to perform, who are the best workers to perform these jobs, and how much it will cost you to employ these workers. Of course, you would have given some attention to these details when you were drawing up your business plan. Now you are ready to act and this chapter is designed to provide you with some useful tools.

Definition

The topics that we will be discussing in this chapter belong to a specialized area of management known as Human Resource Management. Too often in small businesses, a great deal of attention is paid to raising capital, advertising and promoting the business and its products/services, and inventory purchases and control. These aspects of the business should not be neglected, but neither should the employees on whom you rely to accomplish results.

Human resource management (HRM) refers to all the activities involved in the effective utilization of an organization's employees. Its aim is to improve the productive contribution of workers in the organization. Clearly, it is in the interest of all small business owners to enhance the contributions of their employees.

Effective human resource management is much more than hiring people and paying them for their labour services. You have to *manage* workers if they are to make the desired contribution to the success of your business.

Assessing the Need for Employees

Many small successful businesses operate without employees. Sooner or later, however, it may be necessary to hire workers to help you accomplish your objectives. As the business grows, it becomes increasingly difficult and ultimately impossible for one individual to handle all the tasks that must be carried out in running a successful business. Hiring becomes a necessity.

Before you go out and hire an employee, you must determine the answers to the following questions:

- What job is there that needs to be done in the business?

- What skills are required to get the job done satisfactorily?

- How much and what type of experience should the employee have?

- How much training will the employee need?

- What results are expected and what duties will produce the desired results?

- Will the job be full-time or part-time?

- How much are you prepared to pay the employee?

The Job to Be Done

Determining what job needs to be done is an important first step in successful staffing. It makes no sense to hire an accountant if the job that needs to be done is selling. If you need letters typed, then a filing clerk with little or no typing skills will not suit your purpose. The gist of the matter is, you need to know what job you want done before you hire someone to do it.

The Skills Required

Now you know exactly what you want done. You want letters typed because timely and accurate correspondence is vital to the success of your business. Logically, the employee you are seeking must have good typing skills. Ideally, someone who knows how to use the computer to do word processing, using a variety of software programs might fit the bill.

Experience Required

If it is true that experience is a teacher, then other things being equal, the more experience a person has in performing a given job, the more knowledgeable that person should be about the job. A clerk who has just graduated from college will probably not have as much experience and hence knowledge in dealing with clients as an individual who has been on the job for several years. You have to decide whether someone just out of school will be suitable or whether the job really requires someone with more experience. Remember also that salaries will tend to be directly related to experience. More experienced workers are usually paid more than less experienced workers, other things being equal.

Training Required

Even experienced workers need training on the new job. A job at one business establishment is not identical to an equivalent job at another establishment. Each firm has its own way of doing things. You must consider the type of training that will be needed to enable the employee to do the job.

Expected Results

What exactly do you want the job to accomplish? You could, for example, want to increase your sales by 20 percent. Perhaps you could achieve this result by hiring a salesperson to make scheduled calls to customers and potential customers.

Full-Time or Part-Time

If you must hire someone, will it be on a full-time or part-time basis? If you hire a bookkeeper on a full-time basis when, in fact, there is not enough work to keep him/her fully employed, you are simply incurring expenses without economic justification. In that case, perhaps a part-time arrangement would be the better option.

The Pay

Your budget, if carefully drawn up, should be able to help you decide how much you are prepared to pay the employee. You may be *willing* to pay a certain amount, but your budget might tell you that you can't *afford* to pay that much. To avoid future problems, you must decide how much you are willing and able to pay the employee for his/her services.

Job Description

The job description is a useful device for determining your human resource needs. The process of developing a job description will help to answer many of the questions raised in assessing the need for employees. A job description contains:

- ◆ job title
- ◆ department (if applicable)
- ◆ immediate supervisor
- ◆ jobs supervised
- ◆ purpose of the job
- ◆ results expected and duties

It has been discovered that job descriptions are most effective when written in a results-oriented format. Such a format emphasizes expected results as opposed to duties. For example, instead of describing a salesperson's job as:

"calls on clients periodically"

which is duty-oriented, the job could be more effectively described in results-oriented format as:

"serves customers

by

calling on them periodically."

Thus, a salesperson who calls on 50 clients per day without attending to their needs will not have done his/her job.

Finding Employees

Human resource experts use the term "recruiting" to refer to the process of finding employees. Once you know that you need to hire an employee and you have satisfied the hiring pre-conditions discussed earlier in this chapter, then you move on to the next step of recruiting. You can recruit using the following methods:

♦ recruiting agencies

♦ direct advertising

♦ educational institutions

♦ family and friends

In selecting a recruiting method, you will consider the nature of the position, the cost involved in using any particular method, and the budget allotted to recruiting. We shall briefly discuss each of these methods of recruiting.

Recruiting Agencies

Recruiting agencies specialize in finding suitable employees for employers. The advantage of using such agencies is that they have the experience and are familiar with various recruiting techniques. You simply tell them what you need, and they will do the rest. Their job is to recommend the employee. The final hiring decision is yours. The main disadvantage is that they can be costly.

Direct Advertising

You can advertise the job in newspapers, on community bulletin boards, on the radio or on TV. The advantage of this method is the possibility of reaching large numbers of potential employees. The main disadvantage is cost.

Educational Institutions

Schools, colleges, and universities are excellent sources of employees. There are soon-to-graduate people looking for full-time employment, and there are students looking for part-time jobs. The advantage of this method is that it is inexpensive. The disadvantage is that students may lack experience, and students who work part-time may not be able to always meet their time commitments with you.

Family and Friends

This is often the most convenient method of recruiting workers. The advantage is that you will most likely know them and probably what they are capable of doing. Also, they are likely to have an interest in seeing the business succeed. The disadvantage is that family members and friends often have difficulty separating the family and friendly relationship from the employment relationship. A sister might think that it is quite O.K. to regularly take an extra ten minutes at lunch, because, after all, she is your sister.

Selecting the Employee

The recruiting process will provide you with a list of possible employees. The important task is choosing the best candidate for the job. This is often not an easy decision. Volumes have been written on how to select the *right* employee, and there are computer packages that purport to be able to help you to make the right decision.

The most popular selection method used by small business owners is the interview. Before the interview, you should carefully study the applicant's resumé and recommendations submitted in support of the application. It may be necessary to call and speak with the referees.

The employment interview gives you the opportunity to question the prospective employee and glean insights into aspects of the individual that only the face-to-face encounter can reveal. The employment interview gives the prospective employee the opportunity to clarify any issues that may need clarification and allows him/her to decide whether or not he/she wants to work for you.

Some larger companies supplement the employment interview with tests designed to determine competence in a variety of areas. If you use this method, be reminded that performance on these tests does not adequately predict performance on the job.

Typical Questions Asked at Employment Interviews

If you are not experienced in conducting employment interviews, you will find the following list of questions to be quite helpful.

Sample Employment Interview Questions

1. Tell me something about your background.

2. Why do you want to work for this business establishment?

3. In what way or ways do you think you can contribute to our success?

4. What particular skills do you have that might benefit this business?

5. What kind of salary are you expecting?

6. Tell me what you know about our firm and our products/services.

7. What would you consider to be your major weakness?

8. What do you consider to be your major strength?

9. Tell me about your career goals.

10. Tell me why I should employ you.

11. How many hours will you be able to work per week?

12. Will you be able to work after regular working hours?

13. Tell me about your work experience.

14. Have you ever done any volunteer work? Tell me about it.

15. What are your hobbies?

Overview of Successful Staffing

In this chapter so far, we have touched on several areas that you should consider before employing workers. Ending up with the wrong employees can be costly because, among other reasons:

1) it may be difficult to get rid of undesirable workers;

2) recruiting can be expensive;

3) a high turnover of workers means that new workers have to be trained; frequent changes of employees may give the impression that the business is unstable and may thus tarnish the image of your business.

In what follows, we present an overview of effective staffing in ten steps.

Steps for Effective Staffing

1. Define the job to be done as fully and as clearly as possible. A good job description will be helpful.

2. Consider the skills, knowledge, and abilities that are required and recruit the person with those qualities.

3. Obtain references and speak with the referees.

4. Let the employee know what is expected of him/her in terms of results. A results-oriented job description is a good tool.

5. Discuss various human resources policies and procedures, including, for example: hours of work, employment benefits, working conditions, bases of promotion, period of probation, grievance procedure, performance appraisal, vacation and leave, etc.

6. Communicate the organization's mission, philosophy, vision and objectives.

7. Perform regular performance appraisals. Remember that appraisal is a continuous process and not just a once-a-year event.

8. Provide feedback so that your workers know how they are doing.

9. Verbally compliment your workers when they deserve it.

10. Establish a fair disciplinary code and let your workers be familiar with it. Apply it fairly and consistently.

Comment

If you can develop a good working relationship with your employees, and show them that you genuinely care about their personal interests, they, in turn, will tend to do their best to make your business successful.

CHAPTER 8

MARKETING YOUR PRODUCT/SERVICE

∞

Introduction

No matter what else you may do to make your business a success, if you do not succeed in marketing your product/service, you will have no choice but to close shop and say goodbye to the business. It is not an exaggeration to say that good marketing is necessary for business success. If you fail to develop a market for your product/service and maintain it, then all the efforts you've made to secure financing and to staff the business properly will be to no avail.

Marketing is a big topic and many volumes have been written on the subject. Our aim in this chapter is to provide information that will help you to market your business and your products/services in a successful manner.

We begin by defining marketing. It should be clear that marketing, selling, and advertising are not synonymous terms. We will then examine the marketing concept, marketing functions, and the marketing mix in turn. A discussion of marketing methods follows. We end the chapter with a discussion of the marketing plan.

Definition of Marketing

Marketing is a very comprehensive concept. It includes all the activities involved in directing the flow of goods and services from producer to user. Clearly, then, marketing includes such activities as product/service distribution, personal selling, product/service pricing, advertising and promotion, and more.

Economists define a market as a point of contact between buyers and sellers. This view provides some insight into marketing activities. It is obvious from the definition of a market that for a market to exist, there must be a buyer, a product or service, a seller, and a price. An exchange will take place when the buyer and seller agree on a price for the product or service. Marketing is aimed at getting the product/service to the customer at a price that will facilitate exchange and satisfy the customer.

The Marketing Concept

Over the years, the marketing concept has shifted from a product/service orientation to a sales orientation and now to a new concept involving a customer orientation, a profit orientation, and an integration of marketing activities.

According to the new marketing concept, your activities should be geared toward determining what your customers want and then taking steps to satisfy those wants. Profits will likely be generated if you can successfully cater to the needs and wants of your customers. The new marketing concept emphasizes the coordination of all business activities. Even before you begin production or acquiring stock, your customer must be brought into the picture. You must cater to your customers' needs.

Marketing Functions

The marketing activities in which you will be involved as you market your product/service are:

- market analysis
- marketing communication
- market segmentation
- product differentiation
- valuation
- exchange

Market Analysis

The analysis of the market in which you operate is an important step. You must study the market to see what your customers and prospective customers want. You must try to find answers to questions such as these: Is there a demand or potential demand for your product/service? From whom are your prospective customers buying? Is there room in the market for another business? Can you do better than your competitors are doing?

Marketing Communication

Clear communication between you and your customers is extremely important. It is through communication that they will make their wants known, and it is through communication that you will inform them of your products/services. Customers communicate their wants mainly by their buying behaviour in the marketplace. You communicate with your customers through such means as personal selling, advertising, and publicity.

Market Segmentation

Market segmentation is the act or process of separating the market into different categories or segments in order to focus on a particular segment. If you decide on a particular segment that you will try to serve, then that segment becomes your *target market*.

Product Differentiation

Chances are, there will be other firms selling a product or service that is similar to yours. If you can convince customers that your product/service has unique desirable features, you have a good chance of attracting them. Such product differentiation is aimed at developing a preference for your product/service.

Valuation

Your customers will be constantly asking the question: "Is this product or service worth buying?" If they can be persuaded that the benefits derived from the product/service outweigh the cost, then they will be more disposed to purchase the product or service.

Exchange

Exchange (the actual purchase) will take place when you and your customers can agree on the conditions of the sale, including the price to be paid for the product/service. Clearly, the price of the product/service will be an important factor. Other important factors may be the terms of sale (cash or credit), delivery service, convenience (parking facilities or on bus route), cleanliness of the store, behaviour of your staff, etc.

The Marketing Mix

The marketing mix is usually discussed in terms of the four Ps of marketing. These are the variables that you can manipulate in order to satisfy your customers, and they are listed below.

- Product

- Place

- Promotion

- Price

Product Your product is whatever it is that you are trying to sell to your customers. Once you have identified your target market, your product/service must be something that will appeal to them.

Place Your product/service must be available where and when your customers want it. How will you get your product/service to your customers? What distribution channels will you use?

Promotion We touched on the subject of communication earlier in this chapter. What methods will you use to let customers know about your product/service?

Price Price is one of those important factors that can, and often do, determine whether or not your business succeeds. A price that is too low might bring you many customers, but it may prevent you from earning a profit. On the other hand, a price that is too high might chase your customers away. The price that you charge should facilitate the accomplishment of your objectives.

Marketing Methods

Depending on the nature of your small business, you might be able to use many of the following methods to successfully market your product/service. First, we list the methods, then we discuss each one.

- Sales letters

- Brochures

- Business cards

- Yellow pages

- Media advertising

- The Internet

- Cold calls

- Guesting on radio and TV

The Sales Letter

Many different types of businesses have successfully used sales letters to attract customers. The effectiveness of the sales letter derives from its ability to be directed straight to its target. If you are aiming at a particular age group, or professional group, or geographical area, the sales letter is a good instrument to hit your target.

Sales letters tend to be most effective when used to sell products or services of a specialized nature, and products/services that are relatively expensive. For example, if your small business involves selling computer courses to middle-aged business people in the evenings, you may find the sales letter to be an effective tool. If you operate a retail store, a sales letter informing customers of new arrivals may help to draw them into your store.

Brochures

Many small businesses have built up their customer base by using brochures. Bear in mind that if you want your brochure to be read, it should be attractive and well laid out. The brochure should have a compelling appearance that provides an incentive for the recipients to read it. There is little doubt that colour enhances the appearance of the brochure, but colour printing is expensive, so you must weigh the benefit of colour against the cost.

If your brochure is massive (more than 25 pages), it probably will not be read as quickly as one that is relatively small and well laid out.

If you decide to use a brochure, it should specify precisely what product or service you are offering, and explain what it is that sets your business apart from your competitors. For a business that is selling a tangible product, the brochure should contain the following information.

♦ The product that you are offering to your customers. If possible, a brief description should be given

♦ The benefits to be derived from using your product

♦ The nature of your price (competitive, below average, etc.)

♦ Business hours

♦ Your location and/or how you can be reached.

If you are offering a service instead of a tangible product, then your brochure should include the following additional information.

♦ The service or services that you offer

♦ Examples of past work

♦ Your qualifications and experience

♦ Special relevant accomplishments

Business Cards

Many small business owners underestimate the value of business cards in marketing their business. A business card contains information that customers can use if and when they want your product or service. They seem to be particularly effective for professional and technical service businesses, such as lawyers, consultants, florists, car rental agencies, carpet cleaners, auto mechanics, etc.

The Yellow Pages

In the digital age, the **Yellow Pages** has evolved from a printed directory into an online platform, adapting to the changing needs of businesses and consumers. Its role as a marketing tool remains relevant, though it has shifted significantly. While its dominance has waned because of competition from search engines like Google and review sites like Yelp, the Yellow Pages remains a viable marketing tool for businesses seeking a comprehensive and localized digital presence.

Media Advertising

By media advertising, we mean advertising in newspapers, magazines, trade journals, and radio and television. Most small businesses that advertise use the media. If you know your customers and potential customers, you will have an idea of which media will tend to reach them. A brief discussion of each medium is in order.

Newspapers If you are serving the general public, then a newspaper advertisement may be effective since it will have a large total reach. However, if you are serving a more specialized clientele, then a newspaper advertisement may not reach a sufficient number of your potential customers.

Magazines and Trade Journals If you are serving a specialized group of customers, as opposed to the general public, magazines and trade journals may be good vehicles for reaching your target market. A seller of gardening supplies and equipment could do well by placing an advertisement in a magazine that is devoted to gardening. It would be wise for a computer dealer to place an advertisement in a computer journal.

Radio and Television Radio and television are terrific media for reaching large numbers of people. Their big drawback is that they are expensive. If you decide to use these media, you need to be selective in terms of the times and programs that you choose. You can obtain rate cards from these media that will tell you who listens or watches at what time. Again, if you know your target market as to when your prospective customers are likely to be listening to the radio or watching TV, you could more effectively time your advertisements.

The Internet The Internet is a fantastic medium through which small businesses can reach their customers. You can set up your own website, and there are numerous sites where you can advertise your product or service. The downside is that there are so many businesses on the Internet these days that you run the risk of being lost in the shuffle. It may be worth your while to solicit the help of someone knowledgeable about Internet commerce.

One of the advantages of being able to sell your product on the Internet is that you have virtually the whole world as your market.

Cold Calls Cold calls are calls made on prospective customers with whom you have had no previous business contact. It involves physically visiting potential customers either where they work or where they live, depending on the nature of your business. Obviously, this method is not appropriate for every business. However, if you use it, you may be able to clinch a sale on the spot. In any event, make sure that you leave your business card and your brochure if you have one.

Guesting on Radio and TV Being a guest on radio and TV gives you exposure and opens up opportunities for promoting your small business. This is "free" publicity and if the opportunity arises, you can certainly use it to your advantage. If you have a new product or service, you might be able to interest radio and TV people to have you as a guest.

A Note on the Use of Social Media in Small Business Marketing

Social media has become an indispensable tool for small businesses, offering a cost-effective way to reach and engage with a broader audience. Platforms like Facebook, Instagram, Twitter, LinkedIn, and TikTok allow businesses to showcase their products or services, share their brand story, and connect directly with customers. Social media also provides powerful advertising options, enabling businesses to target specific demographics, track performance metrics, and optimize campaigns in real time. Beyond promotion, these platforms facilitate customer interaction, enabling businesses to build trust, gather feedback, and foster loyalty. However, success requires a strategic approach—consistent posting, authentic content, and a focus on building relationships rather than solely pushing sales. When used effectively, social media can significantly boost visibility, credibility, and growth for small businesses.

Your Marketing Plan

Your marketing plan is the document that sets forth how you intend to reach your desired goal. Without it, there is a high probability that you will find yourself in an undesirable position that is some significant distance away from your desired goal.

Given the strategic importance of the marketing plan, you should give careful consideration to its preparation. The following steps should guide you through the process. Like the business plan, the preparation of a marketing plan requires a certain amount of expertise. If necessary, do get some assistance in preparing your marketing plan.

Step 1. Situational Analysis

This step in the market planning process requires a description of the circumstances surrounding your decision to own and operate a small business. Perhaps, for example, you saw an opportunity to satisfy a particular need. This section of the marketing plan should also describe present market conditions, including any possible marketing opportunities that may present themselves in the future. The situational analysis should contain information on the size of the market, its growth rate, its demographic features, pertinent government regulations, and competitive factors.

Step 2. Target Market Identification

In this section of the marketing plan, you specify the segment(s) of the market that you propose to serve. In part, the nature of your business will help to determine your market segment. For example, if your business is a hardware store, your target market would probably be tradespeople, homeowners and maintenance workers.

Step 3. Identifying Strengths and Weaknesses

Having identified your market segment, you must then identify strengths and weaknesses in your product/service. A strength of your business could be the ability to serve customers quickly. A weakness could be lack of resources to expand the current business into other areas.

Step 4. Goal Setting

The next step in the process is the establishment of goals. These goals should be expressed in concrete terms. For example, instead of stating a goal as an increase in profits, it is preferable to state it in more concrete terms such as increasing profits by 10% over the previous year. Your goals could include increasing your customer base by 20% by the end of the next year, increasing your total revenues from repairs by 15%, or adding a new service by a specific date. Remember that your goals and objectives must be realistic.

Step 5. Action Plan

In this section of your marketing plan, you outline the strategy that you will use to achieve your marketing objectives. For example, a strategy could be an increase in your advertising budget by 15% in order to increase your customer base by 10%.

Step 6. Assignment of Responsibility

Here, you specify who will be responsible for the implementation of the marketing plan. The relevance of this step depends on the size of your business establishment. If you are the only one in your firm, then the responsibility will fall squarely on your shoulders. If there are others in the business, such as partners or employees, then the task should be assigned to someone who can perform the task.

Step 7. Budgeting

In this section of the marketing plan, you explain the allocation of funds to the various marketing activities. If financial resources are inadequate to allow for the implementation of the marketing strategy, then the plan may have to be modified or additional resources will have to be found.

Step 8. Progress Evaluation

The marketing plan is designed to help you accomplish certain objectives in a specified period of time. You must evaluate the progress of your marketing efforts in order to determine the success of the plan. This type of monitoring allows you to make any adjustments that may be necessary.

A Final Warning

A word of caution is in order. There are many pre-designed computer packages containing ready-made marketing plans. There are also many business experts who can prepare a marketing plan on very short notice. A marketing plan is a plan to market *your* business and *your* products/services. It should therefore be specific to your particular business, and you should have a significant input in its preparation. Too many marketing plans fail because they are unrelated to the business they purported to guide.

CHAPTER 9

PRICING YOUR PRODUCT OR SERVICE

❦

Introduction

New small business owners often find it difficult to decide on a price to charge for their product or service. As they become seasoned in the business, they tend to become more adept in pricing. As a small business owner, you cannot afford to make mistakes with pricing decisions. We have indicated elsewhere in this book that the price you charge for your product or service dictates, to a large extent, whether or not the business survives.

As a small business owner, you are in business, or plan to get into business, because you believe that you are able to make a profit. A fact that is too often ignored among small business owners is that the pricing of products and services has a direct impact on the profits of the business, and may even determine its overall survival.

This chapter helps you to select from a list of pricing strategies, those that might be practical for your particular business. We begin with a discussion of the meaning of price. We then examine the importance of price, after which, we introduce the concept of the best price. We examine several pricing strategies and practices that you can use and end the chapter with a brief discussion of a reasoned approach to pricing.

The Meaning of Price

Most people would probably define price as the amount of money that a buyer pays to obtain a good or a service from a seller. Expressed in different terms, price is the monetary value of goods and services that are traded in the marketplace. This layman's definition of price is important because it is easy to understand, and it reflects the customers' perception.

You need to pay attention to what your customers think, but in the matter of pricing, it is not your customers, who must make pricing decisions. If they did, you would not have any customers, and without customers, you have no business.

As far as most customers are concerned, there is no difference between price and cost. If a customer pays $25.00 for an item, he/she will often say that the item costs him/her $25.00. And that's O.K. for him/her, but it is not O.K. for you. One of the first things you need to know about price is that it is different from cost, and the difference is crucial. Technically, price refers to selling price, whereas cost refers to the cost of production or the cost of acquiring the item for sale.

The Importance of Price

It is assumed that your objective in starting a small business is to earn a profit. It is assumed further that you will try to minimize the cost of providing the product or service, that adequate marketing will take place, and that other preconditions of profitability, such as excellent service and a trained staff will be attended to. Without these other profit essentials, you will not achieve you profit objective, no matter how efficient you may be in pricing your product or service.

To see just how important the pricing decision is, let us look at the factors that determine profits. These can be reduced to three: price, cost, and volume. Price is what you charge for your product or service, the cost is what you pay to produce or acquire the product or to provide the service, and the volume is the quantity that you sell. It is easy to realize that the price you charge will affect the quantity that you sell. If you lower your price, you will tend to sell more. However, that does not mean that you will make more profits.

Let us look more closely at profits. Profit is the difference between your total revenue and your total cost. We can write a formula for profit as follows:

Profit = TR - TC

Don't be turned off by this formula. It is very simple and quite easy to understand. TR is total revenue, and TC is total cost. If you sell 100 items at $5.00 each, then your total revenue (TR) is $500.00. Now, if you paid a total of $350.00 for those items ($3.50 each), and if you did not have any other expenses, then the formula says that your profit will be $500-350 = $150.

Suppose you had charged a price of $4.00 instead of $5.00. At this lower price, your quantity would increase. If it would have increased to 150, then your total revenue would have been (150 × $4) = $600. If the cost of each item had fallen to $2.80, perhaps because of quantity discounts, your total cost would have been (150 × $2.80) = $420, and your total profit would have climbed to ($600 - $420) = $180. Clearly, price is important.

The price that you charge for your product or service is one of the most strategic elements in the ultimate success or failure of your small business enterprise. It makes good business sense to know how to price for profit.

The Best Price

If your objective is to make as much profit as possible, you should understand that the best price is not necessarily that price that allows you to sell the most units, nor is it always the price that will yield the greatest sales dollars. On the contrary, the best price is the price that will maximize the profits of your business enterprise.

When you set your price, you should consider the cost of your product or service as well as your customers. Costs will help you to establish the lowest price that you can charge, and the demand for your product or service will help you to establish the highest price that you can charge. As a general rule, prices should be high enough to cover costs and help make a profit, but low enough to attract customers and build sales volume.

Pricing Strategies and Practices

If you have been in business for any length of time, it is very likely that you have had to use some kind of strategy. Perhaps you have had to use resources to carry out some activity in response to a move that may have been made by one or more of your competitors. If you are new to the game, you will soon become familiar with many pricing strategies.

Strategy is the utilization or deployment of financial and other resources to accomplish the objectives of the business enterprise in response to active opposition. Strategy can be either proactive or reactive. Pricing is an important selling and marketing strategy.

There are many pricing strategies and practices that are used by businesses. However, we shall concentrate on those that are most relevant to small businesses. These include:

- cost-plus pricing

- target-return pricing

- leader and bait pricing

- bait-and-switch pricing

- odd pricing

- prestige pricing

- promotional pricing

Let us examine each of these in turn.

Cost-Plus Pricing

Cost-plus pricing is certainly the simplest and probably the most popular pricing technique used by small business owners. It involves a mark-up on cost. A mark-up is the difference between the cost of an item and its selling price. If an item costs you $60.00 and you sell it for $100.00, it carries a mark-up of $40.00. The markup may also be expressed as a percentage of the cost. In some cases, the percentage added to costs is based on industry tradition, but in many cases, it is determined by the judgement of the individual small business owner.

One problem with cost-plus pricing is that it does not take consumer demand sufficiently into consideration. A price that is determined simply by adding an arbitrary markup to costs is really a hit-or-miss price. It may or may not result in the accomplishment of your profit objective.

Another problem with this method of setting prices is that it is often difficult to determine what cost concept to use. Should it be full costs, average costs, or direct costs? Sometimes, it is not easy to determine certain types of costs.

Yet another problem with the cost-plus method of establishing price is that it does not sufficiently take into consideration the activities of your competitors and the prices of substitute products. Using the cost-plus method could result in a price that is substantially above or below that of your competitors.

Cost-plus pricing ignores many important factors. Thus, it will result in the best price only by accident. Of course, accidents do happen; but do you want to run your business based on accidents? If you decide to use cost-plus pricing, you should be prepared to make adjustments that bring the resulting price in line with what is acceptable. If the price is not acceptable to your customers, they will shop elsewhere.

Target-Return Pricing

There is no economic justification for the existence of a business enterprise if it does not earn a return on its owner's or owners' investment. Target-return pricing involves setting a profit target, and then setting a price that will attain the target. You could, for example, establish a rate of return of 15% on your investment, and then set out to achieve that target.

In establishing your target rate of return, you must consider factors such as the nature of your business, the degree of competition, the size of your market, your geographic location, etc. If you use this method, the target rate of return should never be set below the prevailing rate of interest.

One problem with target-return pricing is that it does not place sufficient focus on the consumer. Another problem is that the success of this method depends on accurate sales forecasts. If your sales forecast is inaccurate, then your return will be off target.

Leader and Bait Pricing

The 'leader and bait' pricing strategy is common among retailers. You have probably had some experience with it either as a small business owner or as a customer. There are certain products that are quite popular among consumers. These are known as *leaders*. The leader and bait pricing strategy consists of significantly lowering the prices of these popular products (leaders) to attract customer traffic.

The immediate objective is to increase the sale of all merchandise in the store as a result of the increased customer traffic. Once people are in your store, there is a good probability that they will purchase items other than the leaders. If the prices of leaders are reduced below their costs, then the featured items are referred to as *loss leaders*.

The success of this pricing strategy rests heavily on the ability of the leaders to attract large enough quantities of sales of other items. If you use this strategy, you must be careful that loss leaders don't result in absolute losses.

Bait-and-Switch Pricing

Some unscrupulous small business owners, especially if they become desperate, will go to any length to attract customers. They may advertise products for sale at lower than customary prices, even though they have no intention of selling them at the advertised prices. In such circumstances, when customers ask for the advertised products, they are told either that they are out of stock or that the items advertised are of inferior quality. The objective is to get customers to purchase more expensive versions of the items, or to sell them items of comparable quality at higher prices. This is the practice known as *bait-and-switch pricing*. You must be warned that bait-and-switch pricing is both unethical and illegal.

Odd Pricing

It is a fairly common practice among many businesses, particularly in retailing, to set prices in such a way that they end either in an odd number or just under a round number. The assumption is that whether a price is set at 50 cents or 51 cents, the same quantity will be purchased. Therefore, the 51 cents price will bring in a larger revenue.

There is also the assumption that an item priced at $19.95 will have a much more positive effect on sales than if the item were priced at $20.00. The reasoning is that the $19.95 price causes buyers to think of the price more in terms of $19.00 than $20.00.

Note that the effect of odd pricing on sales is based on assumptions about buyers' psychological behaviour.

Prestige Pricing

A lady once told this author that she did her shopping at a particular store all the time. When asked whether the prices there were lower than elsewhere, she unhesitatingly replied, "No, but the owner is such a nice man. He never forgets to inquire about my husband and my kids. He even knows their names." She went on to say that a lot of "respectable people" also shopped there.

It's no secret that many buyers are attracted by considerations other than price. For this reason, some business owners deliberately set their prices above those of their competitors. By so doing, they hope to be able to attract so-called prestige buyers.

By differentiating your products and services from those of your competitors, you may be able to price your products and services above those of your competitors. You must remember, however, that product differentiation involves a cost. Differentiation may be based on such factors as location, product/service quality, and your general reputation.

If you are able to use this method of pricing, you will be able to insulate yourself somewhat from the onslaught of price competition. Any competitor can copy a lower price, but it is a much more difficult task to imitate competition that is based on such intangible elements as service, courtesy, and reputation.

Promotional Pricing

As a small business owner, you may see the need to use promotional pricing from time to time. The objective of promotional pricing is to increase sales volume by giving buyers more for the established price. This pricing strategy can take several forms, including giveaways, premiums, and 'scratch and save.' No price reduction is involved, but the net effect of this strategy is to lower the real price because buyers receive more for the same amount of money.

Promotional pricing is particularly popular in retailing, but it can also be used in wholesaling and manufacturing businesses, especially during periods of inactive sales. It is not quite clear what effect promotional pricing has on profits, but it is quite obvious that an increase in profits will occur only if the business succeeds in increasing its sales sufficiently.

A Rational Approach to Pricing

Earlier in this chapter, we noted that price was a basic element in profits, and ultimately, may determine the success or failure of your small business enterprise. It is highly unlikely that you will obtain all the information that could influence your pricing decision, apply a formula to it, and then come up with the best possible price. Formulas minimize the need for judgement. Nevertheless, judgement does play a strategic role in any pricing decision.

Under certain circumstances, you may find that any of the pricing strategies and practices described in this chapter may be the logical one to use in pricing your product or service, but it is more important to develop a way of reasoning about prices than to adopt a specific formula. The danger is that once formulas are established, they tend to remain in place long after their applicability has expired. Sound reasoning, on the other hand, adjusts to changing circumstances.

A well-reasoned approach to pricing should consider the impact of a pricing decision on total sales volume and total costs. It is easy to see that cost affects price, but you must realize that price also affects costs. Your pricing policy should be concerned with the increase or decrease in the revenues and costs of your business as a whole and not just the item under consideration. If a proposed price change leads to a greater increase in total revenues than costs, the result is an increase in profits.

You should develop pricing guides based on your own costs and on the tastes and incomes of your customers. You can respond to competitive pressures by differentiating your product lines and services, and by meeting the prices of competitors on some items and following an independent policy on others.

Remember that outright head-on price competition is inimical to small business owners. Remember also that sound reasoning in pricing places a premium on managerial judgement, and requires that you pay attention to a number of factors above and beyond the actual costs of the product or service involved.

CHAPTER 10

RECORDS AND
FINANCIAL STATEMENTS

Introduction

One of the essential factors in running a successful small business is the maintenance of proper records and accounts. If you have no knowledge of bookkeeping or accounting, it is well to hire the services of someone who does, so that he/she can set up and maintain an accounting and record-keeping system for you. Although a good record-keeping system will not, by itself, guarantee business success, it will keep you informed and make you aware of the status of your business and reveal weaknesses in operation which, if not detected and attended to, might have serious consequences.

Laws and regulations require that certain information be filed with the government. For example, income tax returns are required by the government, and this provides a great incentive for keeping business records. But accurate records are required also for proper business decision-making. For most micro-business enterprises, an elaborate and complicated record-keeping system is probably unnecessary. The important point to consider is that the system should be appropriate for *your* business. For example, if you do not have any employees, you do not need to set up payroll accounting. Similarly, if you are in a service business that does not carry inventories, you do not need to account for them.

Accounting Records

A session with a competent accountant will help to determine what types of accounting records you need. But it is safe to say that you will need to keep track of goods sold to customers or services provided to clients, you will need records of your expenses, and you will need to keep records of important letters sent and received, contracts, etc.

Although a single-entry system may be used by some small business owners because of its simplicity, it has the disadvantage that it records transactions in one place only. On the other hand, the double-entry system requires that each transaction be recorded in two places. This system provides more information and allows for greater control.

Two important accounting books are the *Journal* and the *Ledger*. The journal or the day book is the original book of entry, and it records the daily transactions in chronological order. Similar items in the journal are entered either individually or as totals in ledger accounts. Because of the double-entry system, the ledger accounts must balance.

To illustrate how accounting information may be recorded, we shall consider the following transactions:

♦ sales of products/services

♦ cash transactions

♦ accounts receivable

- ◆ accounts payable

- ◆ expenses

Sales

Your income is derived from the sale of products or services to your customers. It is important that you keep a record of each sale made. Information on sales is recorded in a *sales journal*. It should include the date of the transaction, the description of the sale, and the amount of the sale. An analysis of the sales journal provides information that can be used for future planning. It also keeps you informed of sales trends and helps you to keep track of your revenues.

Cash

If cash is not properly handled, losses can easily occur. Depending on the nature of your business, you may receive payment in the form of cash, cheques, money orders, and credit card slips. The recording system for cash should be designed to minimize losses. Cheques, cash, credit card slips, and money orders are handled together. Your recording system should provide for the identification of each person who presents payment other than cash. You must be aware that accepting payment by cheque involves a certain amount of risk that there may not be sufficient funds on the customer's account to cover the amount of the cheque. The cheque may therefore be returned with an NSF (not sufficient funds) mark from the bank.

It is good business practice to make all payments by cheque. However, this may be inconvenient for some small businesses, and it may be impractical to make very small payments by cheque. In such circumstances, payment by cash is more economical. An updated chequebook is a useful device for keeping track of your cash position. By adding deposits and subtracting each cheque on the chequebook stub, the chequebook becomes an account ledger. Each cheque is entered in the *cash journal* to indicate the account to which it is charged.

It may be a good idea to establish a *petty cash fund* to pay small bills such as postage stamps, get-well or congratulatory cards, and occasional taxi fares. Each payment from petty cash should be recorded on a form to keep track of the account and the amount paid. The total amount on the petty cash form plus the amount of cash remaining in the petty cash fund should always be equal to the total amount established for the fund. A cheque should be written periodically to replenish the fund, and the expenditures recorded are transferred to the proper accounts in the cash journal.

Accounts Receivable

If you sell to customers on credit, you will usually have some amount of money owing to your business. These debts to your business are called *accounts receivable*. The "accounts receivable" account records transactions for which payment will be received at a future date. Periodically, each customer's account is totaled and an invoice is sent to the customer according to the payment arrangement made. As payments are received, the amounts of the payment are recorded in the customer's account and totaled for entry in the sales and cash receipts journal.

An analysis of the accounts receivable records provides information that is necessary for business decision-making and control. For example, it reveals which customers are in arrears and which accounts need special attention. Obviously, the more credit customers you have, the greater the need for accounts receivable records.

Accounts Payable

In the process of operating your small business, you will normally incur some debt obligations. For example, you may have loan payments, telephone and electricity bills, rent, taxes, wages, and so on. These obligations are *accounts payable*. Such transactions are recorded in a *cash disbursements journal*. In most cases, the vast majority of these payments will be made by cheque.

It is a good practice to organize invoices and bills according to the due date. It is practical to include a "miscellaneous" column in the cash disbursements journal for occasional (as opposed to regular monthly) payments. You would provide special columns for regular monthly payments such as rent, wages, and utilities. An item such as the purchase of a printer is usually an occasional purchase and could be handled in the miscellaneous column.

Expenses

Various types of expenses are incurred in running a small business. You purchase supplies, you buy insurance, and your office machines and other equipment suffer depreciation over time. You purchase a postage stamp today and you use it today. You purchase a filing cabinet today but you will use it for several years in the future. The bases of payments for the costs of operating your small business vary from daily to over an extended period. An accurate assessment of your net income can be made only by determining revenues and expenses for the same period.

There are two bases for computing profit or net income: the *accrual basis* and the *cash basis*. On the accrual basis, adjustments must be made to align revenues and expenses. On the cash basis, items are charged as they are actually paid. A vital assumption of the cash basis is that payments and use occur in the same period. Some jurisdictions specify which basis must be used in certain circumstances. In the absence of such stipulations, many small businesses opt for the cash basis mainly because of its simplicity.

Payroll and Personnel Records

In addition to the records and accounts discussed above, you may need to keep payroll and personnel records. Of course, if you have no employees, you don't have to worry about these records. But with the exception of the very smallest businesses, you will, at some point, hire workers and will be legally obligated to make certain reports to the government.

If you have employees, you should keep a book in which you record the following:

- ◆ the name of each employee
- ◆ the number of hours worked
- ◆ the gross pay of each employee
- ◆ the amount of payroll deductions made

These records are necessary so that you can keep track of employee payroll and you can forward the appropriate amount to the government. You may be able to purchase payroll record books from stationery stores.

It is also a good idea to keep certain types of information on file for all your employees. If your company has enough employees to warrant a personnel or human resources department, then that department will collect and maintain the relevant personnel information. As a minimum, you should have the following information on file for each employee.

- ◆ Full name of employee
- ◆ Current address
- ◆ Telephone number
- ◆ Starting date of employment
- ◆ Starting and current salary
- ◆ Performance appraisal record
- ◆ Attendance record, including punctuality

You should update this information periodically to make sure that it is current.

Financial Statements

The financial information that you have compiled in your records will enable you to produce financial statements. You need to be aware of the financial position of your small business at any given time. It is equally important for you to be able to determine whether your business operations are resulting in profits or losses and to know the magnitudes of these figures. The balance sheet and the income statement will provide information about your firm's financial position and operations.

The Balance Sheet

The *balance sheet* presents a summary of the financial position of the business at a particular date, showing assets, liabilities, and net worth or equity. *Assets* are the physical, financial, and other things of value that your business owns. These include such items as cash, accounts receivable, office equipment and furniture, etc. *Liabilities* are the debts of the business and include such items as bills to be paid, bank loans, and mortgages. *Net worth* is the difference between total assets and total liabilities. The following table illustrates a balance sheet for a hypothetical small service business. Let us examine it.

Assets

In the "assets" section, assets are classified as *current assets* and *fixed assets*. Current assets are those that are likely to be turned into cash within a year. Fixed assets are those that are long-lived and tangible. They include items such as equipment, buildings, and land.

Current Assets include items such as cash, accounts receivable, and prepaid expenses. *Cash* includes cash on hand and deposits in your chequing account in the bank. You must keep a part of your assets in the form of cash so that you can pay current bills. However, since cash is a noninterest-earning asset, it is uneconomical to keep too much cash.

Accounts receivable result from extending credit to your customers. The accounts receivable figure represents the total of all balances owing to you by your customers at the date of the balance sheet. If you offer professional services, you may be able to structure your billing policy in such a way that only a part of your total fee for the service is unpaid while you are providing the service.

Example of a Balance Sheet

A & B Services
Balance Sheet
December 31, 20

ASSETS	
Current Assets:	
Cash	$3,000
Accounts receivable	20,000
Prepaid expenses	500
Total Current Assets	23,500
Fixed Assets:	
Equipment	12,000
Furniture	4,000
Less reserve for depreciation	-1,500

Net fixed assets	<u>14,500</u>
Total Assets	**<u>38,000</u>**
LIABILITIES	
Current Liabilities:	
Accounts payable	$5,000
Bank loans	<u>10,000</u>
Total Current Liabilities	<u>15,000</u>
Long-Term	3,000
Total Liabilities	**18,000**
Net Worth (Equity)	20,000
Liabilities + Net Worth	**<u>38,000</u>**

Prepaid expenses are expenses for items that are paid for in advance of their use. The items are expected to be used up within a relatively short period of time. Prepaid expenses include prepaid insurance and office supplies. They usually represent only a small percentage of the current assets.

Fixed Assets are assets that are tangible, relatively durable (lasting more than a year), and are used in the operation of your business establishment. Examples of fixed assets are computers, factory equipment, delivery vehicles, photocopy machines, fax machines, and buildings.

Liabilities

Liabilities are classified as *current liabilities* and *long-term liabilities*.

Current Liabilities are debt obligations that are payable within a year out of current assets. Current liabilities include items such as notes payable, accounts payable, interest payable, and taxes payable.

Long-term Liabilities are debt obligations that are not due and payable until after one year. Long-term liabilities include items such as notes payable (due more than one year after the date of the balance sheet, and mortgages.

Analysis of the Balance Sheet

The balance sheet provides information that is useful for business decision-making. The most convenient way of using this information is to examine balance sheet ratios. There are numerous ratios that can be calculated from the balance sheet, but the current ratio is one of the most important of these ratios. The current ratio tells how many times the current liabilities could be paid with the current assets. It indicates the extent to which the business can meet its current obligations. The current ratio is calculated using the following formula:

$$\text{Current Ratio} = \frac{\text{Current Assets}}{\text{Current Liabilities}}$$

A current ratio of 2:1 is usually considered satisfactory. In considering the current ratio, you should also pay some attention to the amount of cash available to meet cash requirements within a given period.

The Income Statement

You and others with an interest in your business would want to know how much profit was made from operations during a period of time. You would want to know your revenues and expenses from operating the business. This information is contained in your *Income Statement* or your *Profit and Loss Statement* as it is also called. The Income Statement shows revenues, expenses, and profits for a certain period of time. The following table illustrates an Income Statement for a hypothetical service business.

Example of an Income Statement

A & B Service

Income Statement

January 1 to December 31, 20--

Revenue:	
Income from services	$90,000
Other income	2,000
Total Revenue	$92,000
Expenses:	
Salaries	$20,000
Rent	5,000
Telephone	4,000
Supplies	3,000
Postage	2,000
Advertising	10,000
Travel	3,000
Printing	500
Insurance	500
Miscellaneous expenses	500
Total Expenses	$48,500
Net Income	$43,500

You should prepare Income Statements on a regular basis (perhaps monthly) to provide regular information about the margin of profit that your business is currently making and to track the trend of such profits. In this way, you will be able to take immediate action if the profit margin is falling below what you consider to be a satisfactory percentage of profit (income) from your business operations.

CHAPTER 11

PROFIT PLANNING

Introduction

As a small business owner, you have some business objectives. Perhaps you have set one or more of the following as your business objective(s).

♦ To provide a product or service to your customers and thus earn a profit

♦ To earn maximum profits from your business by satisfying the wants and needs of your customers

♦ To sell as much as possible while earning a satisfactory level of profits

♦ To achieve financial freedom

♦ To survive, that is, keep the business running for a certain amount of time.

Whatever goal or combination of goals that you have selected for your small business, you will certainly have some notion of earning profits.

Without profits, you will not be able to continue in business for any extended time. It can be stated then, that profits are essential for the existence of the business.

Profits are often seen as the residual from business activities. You sell a product or service, you pay your expenses and your taxes, and what is left is your profit. This chapter will show you how you can actually plan your profit.

The Meaning of Profit

The concept of profits that will be introduced in this chapter is probably new to you, but it is the concept that you will need to embrace in your profit planning. The popular notion of profits is the excess of sales revenues from goods and services over the expenses incurred in producing the goods and services. For profit planning, however, this notion is inadequate. The profit concept that is relevant for you is the one that views profits as the excess of revenues from the sale of goods and services over the total cost, including income sacrificed, of producing the goods and services. The following example will help to clarify the difference.

Assume that the following income statement contains the revenues and expenses of your small business.

Hypothetical Income Statement

Revenue:

Sales	$50,000

Expenses:

Rent	$ 2,500
Utility	600

Wages	15,000
Transportation	800
Materials & supplies	10,000
Miscellaneous	500
Total expenses	$29,400

Net Income ($50,000 - $29,400) = $20,600

The net income or profit earned by your business is $20,600, and this is how you would arrive at your accounting profit.

But a more accurate picture of your business is necessary. You would need to know not just the expenses you incurred, but also how much you could have earned in the next best alternative to running your business. In other words, what did you give up? Economists refer to whatever you gave up to run the business as *opportunity cost*. You need to take an economic perspective.

Let us assume that you could have earned $20,600 as an employee instead of investing time and money in your business. Then the situation would have been as follows:

Total revenue	$50,000
Total cost	$29,400 + $20,600 = $50,000
Profit ($50,000 - 50,000)	= $0

In this case, your profit, in an economic sense, would be zero. If, however, you could earn only $18,000 instead of operating your business, then the situation would change as follows:

126

Total revenue	$50,000
Total cost	$29,000 + $18,000 = $47,400
Profit ($50,000 - $47,400)	= $ 2,600

You would then earn a profit of $2,600.

This economic concept of profit is important because it considers the alternative use of resources. It points out that your costs consist not only of direct outlays such as rent, wages, and raw materials, but also interest that you could have earned on money invested in your business, and money you could have earned in other employment.

Planning Your Profit (Income)

Income from your small business operation should not be regarded as a chance occurrence. You should realize that you can plan for profit. In what follows, we show you how you can plan effectively for profit. By planning for profit, you avoid viewing your business income as nothing but a residual over which you have little or no control. You will be shown how you can plan your business operations in such a way that you earn the income that you can reasonably expect from your small business establishment.

Five Steps to Profit (Income) Planning

The following steps indicate the process of planning your income.

Step 1: Establish Your Income Objective

As an independent consultant, you must be able to determine what is a *reasonable* income that you should make from your consulting business. The emphasis on "reasonable" suggests that estimates must be realistic. Your estimate of your desired income may be based on considerations such as the annual income you could have earned as an employee, the interest income you could have earned on the money you invested in your business, and the number of hours you devote to operating your business.

Let us assume, for example, that you would receive a salary of $45,000 per year working for someone else. Let us assume further that you have invested $10,000 in your business and that you could have earned 6% interest on this money if it were placed in a savings account. With this information, you could establish a realistic income objective of $45,600. This figure could be adjusted according to the number of hours you plan to spend at your practice.

Step 2: Determine Your Expected Revenue

The estimate of your expected revenue cannot be pulled out of a magician's hat. It should be based on factors such as general economic trends, the market for your consulting services, trends in your past revenues, your marketing and promotional activities, etc. With this kind of information, you will be able to estimate your revenue for the year. Let us assume that based on the information that you have collected, you can figure out that you could increase your revenues by 10% over last year's figure. If your total revenue for last year was $92,000, then your estimated revenue for the next year will be $101,200 (i.e., $92,000 x 1.10).

Step 3: Estimate the Expenses Necessary to Generate Your Target Revenue

This step requires that you collect expense data for the past year, at least, and then estimate the value of each expense item, making appropriate adjustments. The following table illustrates the process.

Estimate of Expenses

Expense Item	Actual Last Year	Estimated 20--
Salaries	$20,000	$21,000
Rent	5,000	5,000
Telephone	4,000	4,500
Supplies	3,000	3,200
Postage	2,000	1,800
Advertising	10,000	10,500
Travel and accommodation	3,000	3,500
Printing	500	600
Insurance	500	600
Miscellaneous	500	600
Total	**$48,500**	**$51,300**

Step 4: Compute Your Estimated Income from the Figures Determined from Steps 2 and 3

On the basis of the information derived from Steps 2 and 3, the estimated income is:

$101,200 - $51,300 = $49,900

By comparing this income figure with last year's, we note that it is $6,400 more, or an increase of 14.7 percent over last year's income of $43,500.

Step 5: Compare Your Estimated Income with Your Desired Income

The estimated income of $49,900 is $4,300 more than the $45,600 income objective that has been established. If the estimated income was inadequate to satisfy the desired goal, then you would consider some alternatives such as reducing planned expenses, changing your consulting fee, increasing your planned client base by, for example, considering more effective advertising or by improving your company's image. Perhaps you may also need to review your income goal to see if it is realistic. If it is not realistic, it should be revised.

CHAPTER 12

BUDGETING

Introduction

Someone once said that operating without a budget is like trying to drive a car without a steering wheel. The simile is striking. Just as it is wise counsel for individuals to live within their means, so too it is wise counsel for businesses to operate within their budgets. Many small business owners believe that budgets and budgeting are only for businesses of a certain size. They often claim that their businesses are much too small to bother about budgeting. This is a misconception.

In this chapter, we present the budget as a management device that you should use in managing your small business. It will help you to plan and coordinate your business activities in order to achieve desired objectives. The practice of budgeting will expose you to the factors that contribute to the profitability of your small business, and will thus enable you to exert greater control over the course of your business.

Definition of Budgeting

Both individuals and businesses engage in the budgeting process. However, the discussion in this chapter relates to business, rather than personal, budgeting. Quite simply stated, a budget is a plan of action. It is an expression, in quantitative terms, of the path to be followed by the business enterprise over some specified period of time. Budgets are usually made for one year at a time and are therefore considered to be short-term plans. Capital budgets, however, may span up to ten or more years because of the nature of the long-term nature of capital expenditure.

Budgeting can therefore be defined as the process of drawing up and implementing short-term plans that will guide the operation of the business. In drawing up these short-term plans, we assume that it is possible to make fairly accurate estimates of future business transactions.

Advantages of Budgeting

There are many advantages to be derived from budgeting. You must realize that budgeting is not just a sophisticated, time-consuming exercise that is affordable only by larger businesses. In fact, budgeting will help your business, no matter how small it might be. In this section, we will examine a few of the advantages of budgeting in small businesses. Budgeting is not a costless exercise. If nothing else, there is a cost in terms of time, but the benefits will most certainly exceed the costs.

Better Control

Budgeting enables you to have better control over your business. Let us return for a moment to the simile used at the beginning of this chapter, where operating a business without a budget was likened to trying to drive a car without a steering wheel. Without the control that a budget provides, your business could end up being ruined. If you exercise no control over the various categories of expenditure, you could easily end up spending far more than your revenue, and that's a prescription for failure.

Compulsory Planning

We stated earlier that a budget is a plan. Therefore, the preparation of a budget forces you to engage in planning. Without planning, you will not detect future problems, and you will not know what results to expect. Clearly, under such circumstances, you will not be able to take corrective measures to prevent potential problems from developing into serious problems. Budgeting will prevent you from falling into such difficulties.

Greater Profits

The subject of the previous chapter was profit planning. Because the budget forces you to examine closely the various business transactions that you make, you will likely avoid unprofitable transactions. For example, if you increase your sales volume, it may reduce your profit margin. A budget will help you to see the effect of certain decisions on the profitability of your business.

Performance Assessment

Businesses obtain results through their employees. As a small business owner, you may not have scores of employees, but the performance of the few that you may have is crucial to the success of your small business. Your employees will perform better when they know what is expected of them. A budget helps to inform employees what is expected of them. You will be able to compare actual performance with budgeted performance.

Coordination of Activities

The budget is a great coordinating device. It helps to resolve inconsistencies in business objectives. For example, if the production section of your business sets a production target of 200 units per month as its objective, then it makes no sense for the sales section to set a sales target of 250 units per month. A carefully constructed budget will reveal such inconsistencies.

Types of Budgets

There are many types of budgets including, sales budget, production budget, cash budget, operating expense budget, labour budget, administrative expense budget, and materials budget. The list is not exhaustive. The types of budgets that you will need depend on the nature of your business. If your business does not involve the production of goods, then you will not need a production budget. Let us examine each of the types of budgets listed above.

Sales Budget

The sales budget is usually the first to be prepared. It is considered to be the starting point for budgeting because once sales are budgeted, other budgets such as production and materials budgets can be prepared more easily. You will have to decide how much you need to sell during the coming year.

Let us assume that you are in the retailing business and that your sales plan calls for sales of $200,000 per year. You will be able to exert greater control over your sales if you break this figure down into daily required sales. If the number of business days per year is 250, then you will need to sell ($200,000 ÷ 250) = $800 per business day. On some days you will probably sell more than $800, and on other days you will probably sell less than $800. You can similarly obtain weekly or monthly sales averages. If you consistently sell less than $800 per day, then you know that you will not meet your budgeted figure and some adjustment must be made.

Production Budget

The production budget states the number of units that must be produced based on budgeted sales and inventories. The budgeted number of units to be produced can be calculated as follows:

Step 1. Estimate the desired ending inventory of finished goods.

Step 2. Budget sales, in units.

Step 3. Subtract the beginning inventory of finished goods.

The number of units to be produced can be calculated by using the following formula.

Units = desired ending inventory + budgeted sales - beginning inventory

Example. Suppose your desired inventory of finished goods is 100 units, and that you have an inventory of 150 units on hand at the beginning of the period. If your sales budget calls for 500 units, then the number of units you need to produce is calculated as follows:

$$\text{Number of units} = \text{desired inventory} \\ + \text{budgeted sales} \\ - \text{beginning inventory} \\ = 100 + 500 - 150 = 450$$

If you produced 450 units, along with the 150 on hand, then you would have 600 units from which you could sell the 500 units required by your sales budget. This would leave you with the desired 100 units of inventory at the end of the period.

Cash Budget

Every business needs some amount of cash for its normal operation. Without cash planning, you could end up with too much idle cash on hand, or not enough cash to allow your business to meet its normal financial obligations. The cash budget shows the timing of cash receipts and disbursements.

Your sales forecast along with your normal collection period (if your business involves accounts receivable), will give you an estimate of cash receipts for any given period. You must next consider the uses of cash. This information may be obtained from your expenditure plans.

The following is an example of a cash budget for a hypothetical small business enterprise for two months.

Hypothetical Cash Budget

	June	July
Cash at beginning of month	$10,000	$15,000
Receipts	50,000	54,000
Total	60,000	69,000
Cash disbursements	45,000	50,000
Cash at end of month	15,000	19,000

If you were in a position where your cash disbursements exceeded your cash receipts, you would probably have to arrange a loan with your bank. The amount of the bank loan would then be shown as an item in the cash budget and would have been added to total cash. Any loan repayment would be shown as an item in the cash budget and would have been added to total cash disbursement.

Operating Expense Budget

Operating a business means incurring expenses. These expenses should be budgeted and every attempt should be made to operate within that budget. An operating expense budget minimizes the practice of buying on impulse and gives you greater control over your expenditures. An example of an operating expense budget is presented below.

Operating Expense Budget

Item	Budgeted	Amount
Net sales	$40,000	
Cost of goods sold		<u>25,000</u>
Gross profit		$15,000
Expenses:		
Salaries		$6,000
Rent		600
Telephone		130
Office supplies		200
Heat, electricity & water		120
Advertising		1,000
Printing		90
Insurance		120
Miscellaneous		<u>90</u>
Total		$8,350
Profit before income tax		$6,650

Labour Budget

As you will notice from the operating expense budget, labour services represent a substantial portion of total expenses. If you don't plan for human resources, you could end up hiring workers who are not really required and incurring unnecessary expenses. Please refer to Chapter 7 for information about assessing the need for employees. The labour budget forces you to think about real human resources needs and helps you to use your employees efficiently.

Administrative Expense Budget

Administrative expenses include items such as managers' salaries, accounting and consulting fees, legal fees, directors' fees if your business is incorporated, and travel and accommodation. You need to exercise strict control over these expenses because they tend to add up to substantial sums, and because they tend to be ignored because they are not directly related to production and sales volume. You could, for example, budget a certain amount for conference attendance, and then monitor activities to ensure that managers and other administrative personnel adhere to the budget established.

Materials Budget

If your business entails the production of goods, you will most certainly require material inputs to be used in the process of production. The budget for materials should be based on the volume of output you plan to produce. A plan for the acquisition of materials will help to ensure that production will not be halted for lack of material inputs and that large amounts of materials will not be left in undesired material inventories. Of course, your material budget will consider the amount of materials on hand at the beginning of the period.

Budget Monitoring

No matter how carefully you perform the task of preparing your budget, all the benefits will be lost unless you practice budget monitoring. Budget monitoring involves comparing the actual figures with the budgeted figures and then making the necessary adjustments. Indeed, without effective budget monitoring, the budgeting exercise becomes futile.

Let us return to the operating expense budget featured above. We can add two columns in which we show the actual figures and the variance between the planned and the actual figures. This is done in the following table.

Operating Expense Budget with Added Columns

Item	Budgeted	Actual	Variance
Net sales	$40,000	$41,500	+$1,500
Cost of goods sold	25,000	23,900	1,100
Gross profit	$15,000	$17,600	+$2,600
Expenses:			
Salaries	$6,000	$8,500	+$2,500
Rent	600	600	Nil
Telephone	130	135	+$5
Office supplies	200	196	- $4
Heat, electricity & water	120	118	- $2
Advertising	1,000	1,000	Nil
Printing	90	84	- $6
Insurance	120	120	Nil
Miscellaneous	90	100	$10
Total	$8,350	$10,853	+$2,503
Profit before income tax	$6,650	$6,747	$97

In this example, the actual sales figure exceeded the planned figure by $,1500, and the cost of goods sold was less than the budgeted figure by $1,100. This led to gross profits of $2,600 over the budgeted amount. Labour costs turned out to be $2,500 more than the budgeted amount. Was this unavoidable? Did this business hire more workers than were necessary? Was the budgeted figure unrealistic? These are questions that must be answered, and appropriate action must be taken. Notice that the rent, advertising, and insurance figures came in right on target. This could be due to contract arrangements for these items. Variances in the other items were relatively small.

Budget monitoring should take place regularly so that significant variances can be analyzed and corrective action taken before small variances develop into serious problems that can retard the profitability of your small business.

Problems in Budgeting

Budgeting requires discipline. It is painstaking work, but it must be done in order to ensure the success of your small business enterprise. Budgeted figures should not be simply "pulled out of a hat." You should rely on available historical data from your business operation. Go back to your business plan and see how you arrived at the figures there. And do remember to monitor performance and make any necessary adjustments.

There are many problems that you might encounter in the budgeting process. In this section, we point out some of them so that you will be prepared to deal with them when they arise.

Lack of Discipline

Without a certain measure of self-discipline, you will tend to hurriedly put a few schedules together and refer to them as budgets. You must resist this tendency. You must be prepared to spend the necessary time in collecting and estimating the data for your budget. In budget preparation, patience is a virtue.

Inappropriate Budget Period

You must realize that a budget is a control device. If you prepare a budget for an entire year and then compare the budgeted figures with the actual figure one year later, you could encounter severe problems. Failure to select an appropriate budget period is a common problem in budgeting. If you prepare a budget for a year, as much as is practical, you should break down the one-year period into smaller periods such as a month or even a week. This will give you tighter control over your business activities.

Failure to Analyze Variances

Many small business owners behave as if their work is done as soon as they have completed the preparation of their budgets. Little or no budget monitoring takes place. If you don't analyze the variations between the budgeted figures and the actual performance figures, then you will hardly be able to take corrective measures. Variance analysis is a crucial aspect of the budgeting and control process and should not be neglected.

Failure to Take Action

Another problem with budgeting is the failure to take necessary action. Let's assume that you have done a good job of determining the amount of labour that you will require. You operate a retail store and you estimate that your sales will be $25,000 for the period. Your sales volume did not materialize, yet you notice from your budget, that you exceeded your labour budget by a significant amount. You analyze your labour budget variance and conclude that you should reduce the number of employees.

This, of course, is part of the control that budgeting requires. But, alas, many small business owners, for a variety of reasons, find it difficult to take the appropriate action, which, in this case, is laying off some workers. If you want your small business to succeed, you will often be forced to make tough decisions.

CHAPTER 13

PROTECTING YOUR ASSETS

❦

Introduction

Whether your small business enterprise operates as a single proprietorship, a partnership, or a corporation, it is good business sense to protect your assets. By practicing the principles that we have expounded in this book, you will, indirectly, be protecting your assets.

In the first chapter of this book, we noted that small business enterprises are exposed to a high degree of risk. Recall the discussion about the high failure rate of small businesses. Your small business is exposed to a variety of risks such as:

1) the risk of increased competition from new entrants into your market,

2) the risk that the growth of your entire industry may slow down, thus affecting your small business negatively,

3) the risk that the economy may experience a recession, thus reducing your customers' ability to purchase your product/service,

4) the risk of fire, flood or other catastrophic occurrences, and

5) the risk of government legislation that may adversely affect your business.

This chapter shows you how you can take direct measures to safeguard your business assets. In many cases, by protecting your business assets you will be protecting your personal assets as well.

Small Business Risks

The list of risks that your small business faces extends far beyond the short list given above. You may be surprised at the extent of risk involved in running a small business. If you are not familiar with these risks, you will be unprepared to deal with them, and you could end up losing your business and personal assets. Consider how each of the following occurrences would affect your small business enterprise.

(a) Fire destroys your office furniture and equipment.

(b) A thief breaks into your office and takes off with your petty cash, computers, photocopy machines, printers, and other office equipment.

(c) A hurricane or a tornado damages your business property to the amount of $100,000.

(d) Your delivery vehicles are severely damaged by vandalism.

(e) Your office leaks during a heavy rainfall and causes severe damage to your furniture and important documents.

(f) One of your employees sustains a severe injury while at work.

(g) One of your customers injures his/her leg after tripping over an extension cord on your premises and is awarded a liability judgement of $10,000

(h) You lose your business partner through sudden death.

(i) You sustain substantial financial loss because of shoplifting.

(j) You extend credit to many of your customers and thus suffer substantial loss because of bad debts.

Dealing with Risk

The most effective way of dealing with the various forms of risk that your small business may face is to institute a risk management program. Risk management involves plans to deal with potential losses *before* they occur. Instituting a good risk management program entails the following:

1) Identification of potential losses

2) Planning to deal with the potential losses identified

3) Regular revision of the risk management program.

Identification of Potential Loss

The risks to which your small business is exposed must be identified before you can effectively deal with them. These potential losses may be classified as direct losses, such as property damage by fire; indirect losses, such as loss of revenue due to damaged equipment; liability losses, such as losses due to claims or lawsuits against your business; and human resource losses, such as the death of one of your business executives.

Planning to Deal with Potential Losses

Once you have identified your exposure to loss, the next step is to decide how you will deal with the potential losses. Essentially, you will have four options: avoid the risk, transfer the risk, assume the risk, or reduce the risk of loss.

Below, we will discuss good management as a way of avoiding risk and reducing the risk of loss. Assuming the risk involves setting aside money to take care of losses when they occur. Risk assumption is itself risky and not advisable for most small businesses. Instead of laying aside huge sums of money to provide for losses, it may be more practical to transfer the risk through insurance. We will discuss insurance as a way of transferring risk.

Revision of the Program

The potential losses to which your small business is exposed will vary from time to time. As a small business owner, you must regularly review and update your risk management program. For example, the introduction of a new business activity could very well expose you to additional risk, and new legislation and regulations may necessitate changes in your risk management program.

Good Management and Insurance

Even the extended list of possible losses given earlier in this chapter is inadequate to cover the numerous risks that small businesses face. Fortunately, you are not totally defenseless in terms of coping with these risks. As indicated above, you can deal with many of these risks by instituting a good risk management program. In many cases, you can minimize or even eliminate many of the risks. Let us consider good management and insurance as ways of dealing with risk.

Good Management

A good financial plan will enable you to anticipate capital needs, help you secure proper financing, examine the movements of certain key financial variables, and thus avoid financial difficulties. A good marketing plan will help you to carefully study the market for your product/service, study the effect of competition on your business, and provide a suitable reaction to your competitor's move. These are all aspects of good management that will reduce risks.

By practicing good business management, you will be able to avoid or minimize the impact of many of the risks that your small business may face. For example, it is well known that shoplifting is responsible for a large part of the losses sustained by many small business enterprises. Some small business owners respond to this situation by raising prices to counteract the loss from shoplifting. This often has the effect of reducing sales, while not reducing shoplifting. Good management would involve the installation of electronic cameras and/or the hiring of security guards both to deter and detect shoplifters.

Theft by employees has caused many a small business to bite the dust. Theft by employees runs the gamut from taking home small items such as pens, pencils, computer parts, calculators, towels, chocolate bars, and small car parts from the workplace to stealing time by arriving late for work and leaving before the closing time. When such events occur with considerable frequency, they exact tremendous costs on the business. If you suspect that your workers are stealing, then policies should be put in place to check employees before they leave at the end of the work day. An effective system for checking in and checking out workers to ensure that they deliver a full day's work is just good management.

Good management can also prevent or minimize loss that is due to poor credit practices. If your business extends credit, make sure that know the customers to whom you are extending credit by having them fill out a credit application form from which you will gather information such as name of customer, address, date of birth, employment, present salary, bank information, credit references, etc. It might surprise you to know that many small business owners have extended credit to customers whose faces they know only from the fact that they have been frequent patrons. Ensure also, that you run an appropriate credit check before you grant credit.

Do you have a sprinkler system installed? Do you keep properly functioning fire extinguishers on your premises? Have you installed an alarm system? Do employees in your factory wear hard hats for safety? Do you carry out safety checks on your vehicles? Have you secured the entrance to your business premises to make unwanted forced entry difficult? Do you have fire drills periodically? These questions indicate steps that you can take to reduce risk and avoid losses. They are a part of what constitutes good management.

Insurance

Insurance enables you to transfer risks and thus effectively safeguard your business assets from losses that can result from many of these risks. It is a smart decision to use insurance to minimize your losses. The importance of insurance becomes evident when you consider what would happen to your small business enterprise if you were found liable for a substantial sum without relevant insurance coverage.

Claims against you or your business can be a tremendous setback to any small business owner who is not adequately protected by insurance. To operate your small business enterprise without any kind of insurance at all is, to put it bluntly, to flirt with disaster.

Types of Insurance Coverage

There are many types of insurance coverage, and insurance brokers and agents are ready and eager to sell you any of a variety of insurance. It does not make good economic sense to attempt to insure your small business against every conceivable risk. The premiums that you would have to pay would exceed the benefits from such coverage. However, in buying insurance coverage, you should consider, in addition to the protection of your assets, the peace of mind and freedom from worry that insurance provides.

The type of insurance that you will need depends on the nature of your business. An accountant operating out of a small business office with only a secretary would probably need less insurance than a small manufacturer with 10 employees, factory equipment, and a few delivery trucks.

Typically, a small business owner would consider the following types of insurance:

1. Property
2. Liability
3. Theft, Robbery and Burglary

Protection of Property The main type of insurance in this category is probably fire insurance. Depending on the jurisdiction, a standard fire insurance policy may insure you only for fire, lightning, and losses resulting from the temporary removal of assets from your office because of fire. This basic coverage may be broadened by endorsements to include landslides, falling objects, broken glasses, broken water and heating systems, and other such damages to property.

Liability Insurance If a receptionist, a designer, a clerk, or some other employee in your business is injured because of negligence or carelessness on your part, you may be liable for damages. Workers' Compensation may be applicable in some jurisdictions. You will be able to protect yourself against liability for injury to your employees while they are engaged in their duties.

You are responsible for injury or damage to persons or property of others that is due to your negligence. You can protect yourself against damage claims brought against you by purchasing liability insurance. A policy may be arranged to cover all liability risks in connection with the operation of your business, subject to a few exclusions. If you do not require such a comprehensive liability policy, you can obtain one that is tailored to your specific needs. For example, you could obtain a policy that covers tenants' liability, professional liability, and contractual liability.

Theft, Robbery, and Burglary Insurance *Theft* is defined as the stealing of your property. If someone steals your fax machine while it is unprotected, the loss is classified as theft. *Robbery* entails depriving you of your property by violence or the threat of violence. If you were just about to leave your office to go to your bank to make a deposit, and someone holds you up at gun point and relieves you of your cash, such a loss would be classified as robbery.

Burglary is the forcible entry of your premises. If someone breaks down the door to your store and steals your merchandise, or your furniture and equipment, that loss would be classified as burglary. Clearly, these losses can seriously affect your small business enterprise. Insurance can protect against such losses.

Life Insurance

The fact that we have not said much about life insurance should not detract from its importance for your small business. The truth is, you may find life insurance quite useful for your small business enterprise. In certain circumstances, a lender may require that you take out a term life insurance policy as a prerequisite to obtaining a loan. You may be able to attract and keep good employees through the establishment of a group life insurance, and a private pension plan through an insurance company. Other types of life insurance might be of interest to small business owners. It may be well worth your while to pursue the matter of life insurance and how you, as a small business owner, may use it.

Understand Your Policy

This author can recount numerous cases where small business owners believed that they were covered from certain losses, only to be surprised to find that when a claim was made, they were told that their policy did not cover such and such. The actual policy might state something quite different from what the insurance agent tells you. Read the so-called *small print*. Insurance policies often contain terms and phrases that are unfamiliar to the typical small business owner. If you don't understand your policy, get help from a lawyer.

A Final Word on Insurance

In this chapter, we have drawn your attention to what we consider to be some relevant aspects of insurance. Insurance is a very complex matter and we have attempted to make you aware of what insurance can do for your small business in terms of protecting your assets.

We have examined only a small fraction of the various types of insurance. It is unlikely that you will need all the different types of insurance that are available, or that you will be able to afford them if you want them. Since insurance costs money, and since you do not have unlimited financial resources, choosing the types of insurance that are of greatest importance to your small business operation is a matter that requires you to exercise good judgement.

The careful planning and selection of insurance is a necessary step in managing a small business for success. Adequate protection by insurance coverage significantly reduces the risk of business failure, relieves you of needless worry, and gives you peace of mind. It allows you to focus more on satisfying your customers' needs.

CHAPTER 14

CREDIT SELLING

∽∽∽

Introduction

When I was a boy, I recall going into a small village shop. Just over the counter, in black bold letters was a sign that read:

"Trust is dead. Bad pay killed him."

Not very far from that sign was another which read:

"I have credited but to my sorrow,
so buy today and credit tomorrow."

There was no doubt in my mind then that this particular shopkeeper had absolutely no interest in credit selling. Having read those signs, customers knew better than to request credit.

Today, we live in a different world – a world in which credit in business is almost as normal as going to school. The fact is, credit selling increases sales volume. This, of course, is tremendously attractive to small business owners who are interested in increasing their profits, because profits depend on total sales revenue and total cost. Recall the equation defining profits:

$$\text{profit} = \text{total revenue} - \text{total cost.}$$

Notwithstanding the popularity of credit in today's business world, many small business owners still do not extend credit privileges to their customers. That is because there are certain risks involved in extending credit. For example, the customers may not honour their obligations to pay or they may fail to make the agreed-upon payment at the specified time. In this chapter, we will examine the use of credit sales by small businesses.

Types of Credit

There are two main types of credit that small businesses may extend to their customers. They can establish charge accounts (also called open account credit), or they can arrange to accept credit card purchases. Customers who make credit card purchases must first be approved for credit by a credit card company, therefore the risk to the business offering that kind of credit is substantially reduced. We will pay more attention to credit card use by small businesses later in this chapter. Now, we turn our attention to charge accounts.

Charge Accounts

A customer enters a bar owned by a single proprietor. He sits and orders a drink. In 15 minutes, he orders another drink as he engages in trivial discussions with other patrons. Finally, he gets up to leave, telling the bartender, "Charge it to my account." He is able to do that because he has established a charge account at that particular business establishment. The amount of the sale will subsequently be recorded on the books of the establishment. All such charges by this customer will be totalled and entered on a statement that will be sent to the customer at a certain time of the month. Until the bill is paid, it appears on the balance sheet of the establishment as accounts receivable.

Clearly, slow payment or non-payment by charge-account customers can create a serious cash flow problem for the small business owner.

Benefits and Costs

If businesses did not derive any benefits from extending credit to their customers, it is doubtful that they would engage in that activity. It has been established that charge customers buy much more than cash customers at any given business establishment where credit selling exists. There seems to be something in the psychology of buyers that favours credit buying over cash buying. Even in cases where customers can comfortably make cash purchases, they seem to opt for credit purchases.

From the point of view of the firm, extending credit to customers increases their purchasing power, thus making it possible for them to purchase more of the firm's products. Also, many customers find it more convenient to use credit than to use cash for a variety of transactions. For these reasons, extending credit has the benefit of increasing sales.

If the benefits derived from extending credit were attainable without cost, all businesses would engage in credit selling. But many businesses sell only on a cash basis. This suggests that there are certain costs associated with credit selling and that these costs may even outweigh the benefits. Many small business owners have embarked on an unsound policy of credit extension. To their own detriment, they had failed to consider the costs involved. What exactly are these costs? Let's investigate.

What additional costs are you likely to incur if you establish charge accounts? Here are some of them. First, the establishment of charge accounts requires additional record-keeping to keep track of credit sales and customers' indebtedness to your business. This means time and money. Second, there are stationery costs in the form of envelopes, invoice forms, letterheads, credit application forms, etc. Third, there is the cost of postage. This can be considerable if you have a large number of charge customers. Let's assume that you are a Canadian small business owner and that you have an average of 100 statements to send out each month to your charge-account customers. During the course of one year, you will spend in the vicinity of $700 on postage alone. Fourth, you may incur credit collection costs in the form of collection letters, probably written by your lawyer, and charges from collection agencies if the accounts have to be turned over to a collection agency for collection. Finally, once you decide to extend credit, there will be some bad debts that will never be paid.

These costs have deterred many small business owners from extending credit. But the prospect of increased sales is often too tempting for some to ignore. What is required is a good credit-management program if a small business is to take advantage of the opportunities for increased sales made possible by credit selling.

Credit Management

When you extend credit, you do so with the belief that the account will be paid at some stipulated future date. If, not, there would be no logical business reason to extend credit. Before you extend credit, you must take certain precautions to reduce the risk of nonpayment. The fact is, some customers are simply bad credit risks. You must set up a system that will preclude the granting of credit to such customers. Even your regular customers may turn out to be unworthy of credit.

Large institutions that regularly grant consumer credit often use rather sophisticated models to help them evaluate the creditworthiness of the customer. You, the small business owner, may not have access to such elaborate means of evaluating your customers, nevertheless, it is foolish to simply grant credit to everyone who requests it.

In order to insulate yourself against bad credit risks, you should take the following steps:

1. Collect basic relevant information about the applicant. Relevant information would include the following:

a) customer's name

b) customer's current address

c) age

d) marital status

e) number of children

f) employment status, including name of employer and length of employment

g) take-home pay

h) creditors

i) bank information

This information can conveniently be collected by having the applicant fill out an appropriate credit application form.

2. Collect information about the applicant's credit record. There are credit bureaus in most large cities. These and other credit agencies are good sources of credit record information.

3. Establish a credit limit. This should be based on the applicant's ability to pay as revealed by the data collected in numbers 1 and 2 above. It is a good idea to be conservative in establishing the credit limit. This limit may be increased in the future after the customer has demonstrated greater creditworthiness. If the information reveals that the applicant is a bad risk, then credit should be refused. If you must refuse a credit application, explain the reason for the decision and point out to the applicant that you feel it is in his/her best interest that credit not be extended at this time.

4. Carefully monitor all charge accounts, especially new ones, and take appropriate measures to deal with accounts that are in arrears. You should cut off credit from customers who are continually delinquent in settling their accounts, informing them that you will be ready to resume the credit relationship with them in the future when their conditions improve.

No matter how well you manage your charge accounts, some accounts will still be delinquent and others will be uncollectible. When you must cancel the credit privileges of customers, you may lose them forever. Good credit management involves dealing with delinquent accounts in such as way as to minimize your losses while at the same time trying to maintain a cordial relationship with the customer.

When an account becomes delinquent, send a friendly reminder. This could state that you believe that it was an oversight that caused the account not to be paid. Include the original invoice and ask for payment. The reminder could include a statement asking the customer to contact you if there is a problem. It is better to arrange easier payment terms that are manageable than not to collect at all.

If you do not receive any response within a reasonable time (about 10 days), contact the customer by telephone and inquire why payment has not been made. Try to find out when the customer intends to make a payment. If you still do not receive the promised payment, send a letter indicating that the customer's credit standing is in jeopardy and that the account will be turned over to a collection agency or your lawyer in a certain number of days.

If there is no response by the stipulated date, send a registered letter informing the customer that the account is being referred to your lawyer or a collection agency.

This method is clearly time-consuming and expensive. It may cause irreparable damage in the relationship between you and the customer, and it may not be particularly good for public relations. This simply highlights the importance of carefully screening applicants before granting credit.

Credit Cards

Because of the costs and problems involved in establishing and managing charge accounts, many small businesses consider that the costs of charge accounts outweigh the benefits, and hence do not extend credit as a rule. Their position is understandable. Earlier in this book, we noted that small businesses can use credit cards as a way of financing some of their expenses. Here, we show how small business owners can use credit cards to boost their sales.

The acceptance of credit card sales avoids many of the problems associated with charge accounts. Today, customers use credit cards widely. Can you think of a service station, a restaurant, or a clothes boutique that does not honour any credit cards? Credit card sales have become so popular that many merchants now indicate which credit cards they accept by posting notices (usually the sign of the card) at the entrance to their business places.

In order to accept credit card purchases, you must first make the necessary arrangements with the credit card company. There is a charge based on the amount of credit card sales. The mechanical details of credit card transactions need not detain us here. Suffice it to say that small businesses are making increasing use of sales by credit cards.

Despite the credit card company charge, small businesses still find it worth their while to opt for credit card sales over charge accounts. They seem to believe that the costs of establishing and managing charge accounts outweigh the credit card company charge. This is evidenced by the obvious movement away from charge accounts and toward credit card selling. With the increasing popularity of credit cards among consumers, more and more businesses will conduct transactions by accepting credit cards.

CHAPTER 15

ARTIFICIAL INTELLIGENCE AND SMALL BUSINESS

∞

Introduction

Imagine this: You're a small business owner juggling endless tasks—managing inventory, responding to customers, creating marketing campaigns, and keeping track of finances. It feels like there are never enough hours in the day, right? Now, picture having an extra set of hands—one that doesn't sleep, never gets tired and learns faster than you could ever imagine. That's the promise of Artificial Intelligence (AI).

AI isn't just for tech giants or Silicon Valley startups. It's a game-changer for small businesses, leveling the playing field and offering tools that can make your business smarter, more efficient, and, ultimately, more profitable. This chapter dives into how small businesses can harness AI, addressing its benefits, challenges, and real-world applications. By the end, you'll see that AI isn't a far-off concept; it's a practical ally waiting to join your team.

Understanding Artificial Intelligence

Artificial Intelligence might sound like a futuristic buzzword, but at its core, it's about machines doing tasks that usually require human intelligence. These tasks range from understanding language and recognizing patterns to learning from data and making decisions. For small businesses, AI means tools that simplify your work, anticipate your needs and even help you connect better with customers.

Let's break it down:

- **Machine Learning**: Imagine teaching a machine to learn from data, so it keeps getting better at tasks like predicting sales trends.

- **Natural Language Processing (NLP)**: Think about tools like chatbots that can have a real conversation with your customers, answering their questions in seconds.

- **Predictive Analytics**: Ever wish you had a crystal ball? Predictive analytics uses past data to give you insights about the future, helping you make smarter decisions.

- **Automation**: This is where AI shines—taking repetitive tasks off your plate so you can focus on growing your business.

These technologies aren't just for tech-savvy experts. Today, AI tools are user-friendly and designed with small business owners in mind.

The Benefits of AI for Small Businesses

AI can feel like having a superpower for your business. Let's explore how it can transform your operations:

Streamlining Operations

Think of all the repetitive tasks you do daily—inputting data, tracking inventory, scheduling meetings. AI can handle these tasks with speed and accuracy, freeing you to focus on strategy and creativity.

Enhancing Customer Experience

Your customers expect quick, personalized responses. AI-powered chatbots can handle this, answering questions, taking orders, and even making recommendations 24/7. Imagine the loyalty you could build with that level of service.

Smarter Decision-Making

Running a business often means making decisions with incomplete information. AI analyzes your data—sales trends, customer behaviour, market changes—and turns it into actionable insights. It's like having an expert advisor always on call.

Cutting Costs

AI can reduce errors, optimize workflows, and automate processes, all of which save money. For instance, tools that monitor equipment can predict maintenance needs, reducing costly downtime.

Staying Competitive

In today's fast-paced market, small businesses need every advantage. AI helps you offer high-quality services efficiently, keeping you on par with larger competitors.

How Small Businesses Are Using AI

Now that we've covered the benefits, let's look at how small businesses are putting AI to work:

In Marketing

AI helps small businesses punch above their weight when it comes to marketing. Tools analyze customer data to create targeted ads, recommend products, or even automate social media posts. You're not just advertising; you're connecting with your customers in meaningful ways.

In Sales

Ever wonder which products to promote? AI-powered sales tools analyze purchasing patterns and suggest upselling or cross-selling opportunities. It's like having a personal sales assistant who knows your customers inside and out.

In Operations

Managing inventory is a challenge for any small business. AI tools track stock levels, predict demand, and even automate reordering, ensuring you're never out of a best-seller—or stuck with excess inventory.

In Customer Support

Small businesses thrive on customer satisfaction. AI chatbots handle basic inquiries instantly, while you and your team focus on building relationships and solving complex problems.

In Financial Management

Keeping track of finances can be daunting. AI-powered bookkeeping tools categorize expenses, forecast cash flow, and even flag potential fraud.

Overcoming the Challenges of AI

While AI offers incredible opportunities, integrating it into your business comes with hurdles:

- **Cost**: Some AI tools require upfront investment, but many scalable options are budget-friendly.

- **Learning Curve**: Like any new tool, AI takes time to master, but most platforms are designed to be intuitive.

- **Privacy**: Handling customer data responsibly is critical. Make sure your AI tools comply with data protection laws.

- **Resistance to Change**: It's natural to be skeptical. Start small and demonstrate the value of AI to build confidence.

The Future of AI in Small Business

AI is constantly evolving, and its role in small businesses will only grow. Imagine voice-activated search optimization for your website, AI tools that help you achieve sustainability goals, or systems that personalize every customer interaction.

The key is to stay curious and proactive. The businesses that embrace AI today are the ones that will lead tomorrow.

Conclusion

Artificial Intelligence isn't a luxury for big companies—it's a tool that empowers small businesses to achieve their full potential. By automating tasks, enhancing customer experiences, and providing insights that drive smarter decisions, AI helps you work smarter, not harder.

So, take the leap. Start small, explore the tools available, and watch as AI becomes a partner in your business's success story. With AI, you're not just keeping up with the competition—you're setting the pace.

CHAPTER 16

SMALL BUSINESS RESOURCES ON THE INTERNET

Introduction

The Internet and the World Wide Web have opened up numerous opportunities for small businesses. Many of the small businesses that have been established within the past few years have been Internet-related. The concept of e-commerce has special significance for small businesses. The Internet and the web have expanded marketing opportunities that were unthinkable only a few years ago. Certain small businesses now have access to international markets via the Internet. Depending on your particular line of business, you may be able to sell your products/services to an international clientele.

But whether or not your business is such that the Internet gives you access to customers worldwide, you will still find the Internet a veritable source of information that is pertinent to your small business enterprise. There are literally millions of pieces of information related to small businesses on the Internet.

Granted, not all of them will be useful or practical for all small business owners, and to access the information that may be useful to you, you will need access to a computer hooked up to the Internet. If you don't have access to a computer with Internet connections, there are places where you can pay a small price to use such facilities.

Searching for information on the Internet is time-consuming, and not too many small business owners would find it practical to devote all that time to searching for information. Therefore, this chapter presents several sites that you, the small business owner, will find helpful. To enhance the usefulness of the chapter, we have provided an annotated list of resources.

You should not attach any significance to the order in which the information is listed. You must bear in mind also, that information on the Internet changes rather quickly. We have, however, listed sites that contain information that will be usually relevant to your small business enterprise.

RESOURCES FOR SMALL BUSINESSES

For All Countries

1. **Google My Business** (business.google.com) – Helps businesses improve local search visibility.

2. **LinkedIn** (linkedin.com) – Networking and marketing for professionals.

3. **Canva** (canva.com) – Easy-to-use graphic design tools for marketing.

4. **HubSpot** (hubspot.com) – CRM and marketing tools for small businesses.

5. **Shopify** (shopify.com) – E-commerce platform for selling online.

Canada

1. **Canada Business Network** (canada.ca) – Government resources for small businesses.

2. **BDC (Business Development Bank of Canada)** (bdc.ca) – Financing and advice for small businesses.

3. **CFIB (Canadian Federation of Independent Business)** (cfib-fcei.ca) – Advocacy and support for small businesses.

4. **CRA (Canada Revenue Agency)** (canada.ca/cra) – Tax information and programs for businesses.

5. **Futurpreneur Canada** (futurpreneur.ca) – Support for young entrepreneurs.

United States

1. **SBA (Small Business Administration)** (sba.gov) – U.S. government support for small businesses.

2. **Score** (score.org) – Free mentoring and resources.

3. **IRS (Internal Revenue Service)** (irs.gov) – Tax resources and business structures.

4. **U.S. Chamber of Commerce** (uschamber.com) – Advocacy and business services.

5. **Small Business Trends** (smallbiztrends.com) – News and tips for small businesses.

United Kingdom

1. **Gov.uk** (gov.uk/business) – Official government business resources.

2. **FSB (Federation of Small Businesses)** (fsb.org.uk) – Support and advocacy for small businesses.

3. **Companies House** (gov.uk/companies-house) – Business registration and records.

4. **Startups.co.uk** (startups.co.uk) – Advice for starting and running businesses.

5. **UK Finance** (ukfinance.org.uk) – Financial advice and resources.

Australia

1. **Australian Business Register (ABR)** (abr.gov.au) – Business registration and ABN lookups.

2. **Business.gov.au** (business.gov.au) – Comprehensive government resources.

3. **ATO (Australian Taxation Office)** (ato.gov.au) – Tax guidance for businesses.

4. **Fair Work Ombudsman** (fairwork.gov.au) – Workplace rights and regulations.

5. **COSBOA (Council of Small Business Organisations Australia)** (cosboa.org.au) – Advocacy for small businesses.

Industry-Specific and General Resources

1. **QuickBooks** (quickbooks.intuit.com) – Accounting software.

2. **Xero** (xero.com) – Cloud-based accounting solutions.

3. **Eventbrite** (eventbrite.com) – Tools for event management.

4. **Weebly** (weebly.com) – Website creation for small businesses.

5. **Mailchimp** (mailchimp.com) – Email marketing solutions.

GLOSSARY OF COMMON BUSINESS TERMS

This glossary of common business terms provides a convenient reference for the small business owner. It contains many of the terms found in the book, but it also contains many business terms that are not mentioned in the book.

A

Accelerated depreciation: depreciation at a rate faster than usual.

Accident insurance: a policy that allows for payment of a stipulated sum in the event of injury or accidental death.

Account: a statement showing debit and credit entries.

Accountant: a trained professional who analyses and reports business or organizational financial transactions.

Accounts payable: amounts owed by a business because of normal business transactions. An example would be unpaid bills for supplies.

Accounts receivable: amounts owing to a business because of normal business transactions. An example would be the amount due to a business for credit sales.

Accrual basis: a system of allocating revenue and expense items on the basis of when the revenue is earned or the expense incurred rather than when the cash is received or paid out.

Act of God: an event such as hurricane or natural flood that is beyond human control.

Ad valorem: based on value rather than on weight. For example, an ad valorem tariff is one that is based on the value of the item rather than on its weight or quantity.

Advertising: any paid form of nonpersonal presentation and promotion of goods or services.

Agent: one who acts on behalf of another in transactions with a third party.

Alien corporation: a corporation doing business in one country but chartered in another.

Amalgamation: the merging or integration of two or more business concerns.

Amortize: to reduce or liquidate by installment payments.

Annuity: a series of payments over a specified number of years.

Appraisal: the process of evaluating an employee's job performance.

Appreciation: an increase in value over a period of time.

Asset: anything of value that is owned by an entity.

B

Balance sheet: a statement of assets and liabilities on a specific date.

Balloon payment: a final lump sum payment made to liquidate a financial obligation.

Bear market: a market in which prices are falling.

Bill of sale: a certificate of transfer of property from one owner to another.

Blue chip: a term used to describe stocks or companies that are of high quality.

Bond: a certificate of indebtedness of the issuer to the holder.

Book value: the value of an asset as recorded on the company's books.

Brand: a mark (trade-mark) that identifies a product.

Break-even point: the point at which total revenue is equal to total cost so that profits are just zero.

Budget: a plan for future revenues and expenditures during a specified period of time.

Bull market: a market in which prices are rising.

Burglary: forcible entry to take property unlawfully.

Business cycle: ups and downs in business conditions over a period of time.

Business plan: a carefully drafted plan of action for a business to ensure the achievement of its objectives.

C

Capital: equipment, machinery, and money.

Capital asset: a long-term asset that is not bought and sold in the ordinary course of business.

Capital stock: the shares of the owners of a corporation.

Cartel: an association of firms whose purpose is to control the market for a particular product.

Cash basis: a system in which income and expenses are recognized only at the time when cash is received or paid out.

Cash flow: the actual flow of dollars into or out of a business.

Certified cheque: a cheque that is guaranteed by a bank as to signature and adequacy of funds.

Chattel mortgage: a mortgage on personal property other than real estate.

Collateral: security of some sort given to a creditor to guarantee payment.

Common stock: ownership shares in a corporation. Common stock holders are the last to receive any distributions of earnings.

Consumer credit: credit extended to consumers to encourage sales.

Corporation: a form of business organization in which shareholders have limited liability. The corporation has the power to act as an individual.

Cost-benefit analysis: the process of weighing and comparing the costs and benefits of a project to aid in the decision making process.

Credit: the ability to obtain goods/services with a promise to pay later.

Creditor: person or organization that has lent money.

Current assets: assets that can be converted to cash within a relatively short time.

Current liabilities: a debt that is expected to be paid within a relatively short time.

Current ratio: the ratio of total current assets to total current liabilities. It is a measure of liquidity.

D

Dead stock: inventory whose demand has fallen to almost zero.

Debenture bonds: bonds secured by the creditworthiness of the borrower.

Debit: an accounting entry causing an increase in an asset or a decrease in a liability.

Default: failure to meet an obligation at a stipulated time.

Direct costs: expenses that can be directly identified. Direct outlays such as material and labour costs.

Disposable income: personal income remaining after all taxes have been paid.

Diversification: producing or carrying a wide variety of products or engaging in many different business activities.

Dividend: the part of a corporation's profit that is to be paid out to its shareholders.

E

Entrepreneur: one who organizes a business enterprise and incurs the risks.

Equity: the net worth of a business.

Equity capital: capital acquired from investors without obligation to repay. The investors accept shares in the business.

Exchange rate: the rate at which one country's currency exchanges for that of another.

F

Feasibility study: a study designed to determine whether an idea or a business has a good chance of success.

Fiscal year: the 12-month period used by a business to indicate its year.

Fixed assets: assets of a business such as buildings, machinery, and equipment that are expected to last for a long time and that will not be converted into cash within a year.

Fixed costs: these are costs that do not change as the volume of production changes. Salaries and rent are examples.

Fixed liabilities: debts that are not due for a least a year.

Franchise: an exclusive right given to someone to perform a stipulated business activity in a specified area.

G

General partnership: an arrangement whereby two or more people agree to engage in business as owners. Each co-owner has unlimited liability.

Goodwill: the difference between that price paid for a going concern and its book value is taken as a measure of goodwill. It is an intangible asset.

Gross domestic product: the market value of all goods ans services produced in a country during a year.

Gross margin: net sales minus cost of goods sold.

H

Hidden asset: an asset that is carried on the books of a business at much less than its fair market value.

Holding company: a corporation whose purpose is to own the common stocks of other companies.

Horizontal merger: the amalgamation of separate companies engaged in the same business activity.

I

Implied warrantee: a warrantee that is implied by law, though not explicitly stated.

Income statement: a financial statement showing revenues, expenses, and net income during a period of time.

Industrial goods: products used by businesses in manufacturing other goods.

Inventory: stocks of finished or semi-finished goods.

Investment portfolio: a list of securities owned by an individual.

J

Job description: a written statement of the duties and responsibilities of an employee.

Job specification: a statement of the personal and other qualifications required to perform a job satisfactorily.

L

Leverage: the use of external funds to earn profits.

Liability: a debt owed by a business enterprise.

Limited liability: a condition whereby an investor is liable only to the extent of his/her investment in the business.

Line of credit: an arrangement between a financial institution and a borrower whereby the borrower can borrow up to a stipulated amount.

Liquid asset: an asset that can be converted into cash without much loss.

Liquidity: the ability to meet upcoming debt obligations.

M

Market: a meeting point between buyers and sellers.

Marketing: the various activities involved in directing the flow of goods and services from producers or sellers to the final users.

Marketing plan: a detailed plan outlining how the business will get from where it is to where it wants to be.

Market segmentation: dividing a market into different sub-markets or segments that have similar characteristics.

Markup: an amount or percentage added to the cost price to arrive at the selling price.

Mission statement: a statement of the primary purpose for the existence of the business.

Mortgage: a loan secured by property.

N

Net profit: operating profit minus income taxes.

O

Owners' equity: assets remaining after all creditors have been paid off.

Overhead: all business costs except direct labour and materials.

P

Partnership: a business formed by two or more persons who agree to be co-owners of the business.

Partnership agreement: an agreement, usually written, detailing the terms under which the partnership will operate.

Preferred stock: a stock that has certain preferences over common stock.

Price lining: the practice of selling a class of merchandise in a limited number of price categories.

Product differentiation: a market situation achieved by making similar products appear to be different.

Promotion: efforts such as advertising and other activities aimed at increasing sales.

Proprietorship: a business owned and operated by a single owner. It is also known as a single or sole proprietorship.

Q

Quick assets: assets that can be readily converted into cash without appreciable loss.

R

Retailer: a business that buys goods for resale to the ultimate consumer.

Retained earnings: profits that have not been distributed to shareholders, but retained by the company. Also called *undistributed profits*.

Risk: the probability of suffering a loss.

Risk management: taking steps to prevent losses before they occur.

S

Serial bonds: bonds issued at the same time but with different maturity dates.

Shareholder: the holder of a share certificate certifying part ownership of a corporation. Also called stockholder.

Silent partner: a co-owner of a partnership who takes no active part in managing the business.

Slow asset: an asset that will take a long time to be converted into cash.

Sole proprietorship: see *proprietorship.*

Speculation: the act of buying and selling with the hope of making a profit from changes in prices.

Spot price: the price of goods for immediate delivery.

Stakeholder: anyone who has financial or other interests in a business.

Stockbroker: an agent who buys and sells stocks and bonds.

Stock dividend: a dividend paid in the form of stock.

Subventions: grants and subsidies.

Surtax: a tax imposed over and above the usual tax.

T

Target market: the section of the total market selected for special attention or treatment.

Target pricing: a pricing technique designed to produce a 'target' rate of return. Also called *target-return pricing.*

Tax avoidance: legal means of avoiding taxes.

Tax evasion: illegal means of avoiding taxes.

Trade credit: debt arising from credit sales between firms.

Trademark: a distinctive sign or mark that readily identifies a company or its products.

U

Undercapitalized: with insufficient funds to carry on the current scale of operation.

Undistributed profits: see *retained earnings*.

Union label: a label indicating that the product was made with unionized labour.

Unlimited liability: a condition whereby a person is fully liable for all debts incurred by his/her business, even to the extent of personal belongings.

V

Variable costs: costs that vary with the volume of goods produced. They include items such as labour and materials.

Venture capital: an external source of financing for business ventures.

Voting stock: a stock that gives the owner the right to vote at corporate meetings.

Voucher: a document showing that a certain payment is in order and has been authorized.

W

Warranty: a promise by a seller that the good or service will fulfil a stated requirement during a stipulated time period.

Wholesaler: a middle-person who buys merchandise for resale to retailers and other merchants.

Working capital (net): the difference between current assets and current liabilities.

www.ingramcontent.com/pod-product-compliance
Lightning Source LLC
Chambersburg PA
CBHW040854210326
41597CB00029B/4841